KEEP ON C N

The Life Story of Ernest Hicks
1912–2007

By JOAN HICKS

Published by 'Mitzicat', High Street, Blockley, Moreton-in-Marsh,
Gloucestershire. GL56 9HF

First Published: 2024

British Library Cataloguing in Publication Data
A catalogue record for this book is available from the British Library

ISBN 978 1 3999 7371 7 (print)

Printed in the United Kingdom by Henry Ling Limited, at the Dorset Press, Dorchester, DT1 1HD

Authors Notes

'Keep On Going On' may seem an odd title for the life story of my Father but it sums up his philosophy on life.

Whenever, I was faced with a difficult decision or some other of life's adversities, he would always put his hand on my shoulder, look directly at me and say: 'Keep on Going on, My Dear', 'Keep on Going on'.

His kind words have kept me going in times when difficult decisions have had to be made and continue to do so to this day..

This work has not been extensively edited. I have been anxious to write as far as possible using my Father's own words (shown in italics) and to try to capture the flavour of the unique characteristics of the time in which he lived.

I am grateful to my cousin Dorothy Powers (nee Hicks) for keeping me on track and giving me encouragement when needed.

With thanks to the Blockley Heritage Society for sourcing original photographs.

The manuscript for this book and a copy of the printed book will be placed with the Worcestershire Archives and copies also given to the Blockley Heritage Society.

With thanks to Andrew Hopwood of Henry Ling Ltd. Printers, for his help and assistance in getting this work published.

Joan M. Hicks
22 October, 2023

CONTENTS

LIST OF ILLUSTRATIONS

Foreword

This is the story of my Father. Ernest (Ernie) Hicks, also nicknamed 'Skimp' by his brothers. It reflects a life of humour, adversity and stoicism from a young age and throughout his life. An accident at a very early age left a disability which would have consequences throughout his life.

I spent many a happy hour sitting with him as he recalled his life experiences both as a child and through till his death. His stories were spellbinding. Stories about his life, his work and the life of his parents. I have also been able to retain notes in his own hand which will be used in the narrative. His life spanned a period of rapid social and technological change and two World Wars that affected the lives of the population of Great Britain in many ways.

My Father did not serve in WWII because of his disability. His Father (John 'Jack' Hicks) served in the First World War and this undoubtedly, not only changed the course of his Father's life but also that of his son, my Father, Ernest.

I do not think the Story would be complete if I did not include all the information that I have found about my Mother, Doris Annie Hicks, nee Moore, always called 'Dora'. My Mother was placed in a children's home at an early age by her Mother, my Maternal Grandmother, Caroline Annie Moore. My Mother never knew her family.

I am deeply indebted to my Father for the amount of information that he wrote down about his life and the life and times of those around him. I believe that a unique story has been created about the times he lived in that I hope will be read for many generations to come.

Joan M Hicks
22nd October, 2022

Ernest Hicks aged about 10. Photograph taken at Blockley Boys School.

PART I
SEZINCOTE ESTATE

My Grandfather and Grandmother moved to Sezincote Estate in the Parish of Bourton on the Hill, from The Green, in Moreton-in-Marsh, where my Grandfather had worked on Blenheim Farm as a Carter. They moved to Sezincote between April 1911 and when my father Ernest Hicks was born on 22nd October 1912.

My Grandparents already had three live children, Bill (William George Hicks), born on 1st October, 1904; George Thomas born on 25th October 1905; and Annie Elizabeth ('Our Lizzie') born in July, 1907.

My Father was my Grandmother's fifth child. She had lost a baby, Albert Edward, born in 1909. She always referred to him, sadly, as 'little Bertie', who died at the age of about one year and is buried in St. Mary's Church Cemetery at Icomb where his Paternal Grandparents are also buried.

Granny Willett from Great Rissington aged about 90

My Grandmother had one more child after my Father, in 1915, John, christened Arthur John.

My Father describes what he was told by his mother about his birth:

"I was born on October, 22nd 1912 between the hours of 4–5 a.m. at the Sezincote Estate Cottages, (now one cottage called Tuckwell's Lodge along Sezincote Lane) *under the watchful eyes of Dr. Yelf, of Moreton-in-Marsh GP Practice. Also, my Granny Willett* from Great Rissington. I was told years later by my mother that my Father had to (at 4 a.m.) walk all the way from the Cottage to the Moreton-in-Marsh House of Dr Yelf to ask if he would come to Mother. Dr. Yelf came on horse-back with his medical case to attend Mother. She told me, years later, that I was a very big Baby. The biggest child born in our family".* The children liked Granny. She was kind and sent them cakes *'made with all sorts of fat and fruit'.*

*Granny Willett nee Marlow, nee Caddel from Great Rissington came to look after the children during her daughter's confinement. She came on several occasions over the years to help out with the children.

My Father said they '*even found pieces of onion in the cake, but it was cake and they really looked forward to it*'. She also sent other food, and much treasured six-pences sewn to cards for birthdays. Father said she '*wrote as she spoke*' and her words and sentences were all joined up.

Equally, they also liked their Grampy Willett. Who also was very kind.

Granny and Grampy Hicks taken at Icomb with their youngest son Albert Edward.

His Paternal Grandmother, Granny Hicks, nee Watson. Her Christian name was Lucy, was certainly not liked by the children. She was very strict and Father said, they would, as a consequence, play her up. Grampy (George) Hicks was equally feared.

My Father recalls that he went over to Icomb with his Father, John (Jack) Hicks and the pony called 'Jimmy' and trolley they owned. John Hicks told Father to let the pony graze the verge but this did not suit Grampy George. He ordered John to 'get that pony off the grass', so my Father had to take the pony further down the lane and wait for his Father, John.

LIFE ON SEZINCOTE ESTATE – THE EARLY YEARS

My Father remembers his early years as very happy. As Head Carter at Sezincote, my Grandfather was entitled to a tied cottage. At the time what is now known as Tuckwell's Lodge was two cottages and Shepherd Tidmarsh and his family occupied the other half. My Father was born in the bedroom of the cottage in the side shown in the photograph below:

Tuckwell's Lodge as it is today. (A Cedar tree is shown in the photograph. It was only cut down in the 2020's)

When he was still a toddler, Shepherd Tidmarsh's son, Wes Tidmarsh, was playing with my Father under the big cedar tree that used to stand at the side of Tuckwell's Lodge. Being the bigger boy, Wes Tidmarsh pushed my Father over and he fell on a broken jam-jar and badly cut his forehead, just above his eye.

'It was when I was between the age of 15 months to 2 years of life that Mother and Dad's troubles concerning me was experienced. Again, when I was playing with my brothers and Sister, and also the neighbour's children, I was deliberately pushed over, from which I received a deep cut just above my right eye from a broken jam jar which needed an amount of stitches into the deep cut at the Moreton Surgery from Dr. Yelf.'

He had that scar for the rest of his life – and Wes Tidmarsh got the walloping of his life!

My Father also had a round hat given him which he is shown wearing on a photograph taken by the gate at Tuckwell's Lodge with the rest of the family (the gate is still there). This hat one day was blown off into a pig sty and my Father's brother George retrieved it for him. My Father had a name for the hat, he called it his 'Gargydoor'.

My Grandmother made most of the clothes for her children as she was a good needlewoman and continued to make the family clothes. Father remembers: In the early 1900s both younger boys and girls wore little dresses and he is shown dressed in this manner in the photograph below.

Centre: Jack Hicks holding Ernest; Lizzie on right and William left with George next to his Father. This photograph is taken by the gate next to Tuckwell's Lodge. As of 24th January, 2017 this gate still exists.

Father remembers:

'Now when a new pair of little trousers had to be made for either me or brother John, Mother used to get an old pair of men's trousers, or jacket, take them apart and wash them. Then she used to get out her sewing machine together with a paper pattern and make new trousers for us. There was often one thing she forgot to do after completion of the making and handing them to the wearer. Therefore, when the trousers were being worn there was a small prickly feeling up around the space between one's legs, where some of the small tender places are attached. When it was explained to Mother that something was sticking in those tender places her reply was to 'take the trousers off'. Therefore, on inspection it was found that a pin had been left in, just where the trousers were joined in middle, therefore after the offending object had been removed, all was O.K. again.

The cottage at Tuckwell's lodge was becoming too small for the growing family and my Grandfather requested a move to a bungalow that had become available in the Poultry Yard. *"it was due to the size of our family, living in a very small house and also Father being the Estate's Head Carter, Father took it upon himself to ask if he could be moved further down into the Estate where there was an empty house in the Poultry Compound. This was agreed upon by old Colonel Dugdale".*

I gathered that the move to the Poultry Yard was also better for my Grandfather's work as it was closer to where the Estates horses were stabled and my Grandmother then worked in the Dairy making cream and butter and looking after the fowl in the poultry yard. Depending on the time of year and whether Captain and Lady Dugdale were in residence at Sezincote or in London, the produce used to be sent to them in London and also sent to their friends around the country.

THE POULTRY YARD, SEZINCOTE

My Father writes*: It was at that time when I was about 24 months to 3 years old that we moved to the Poultry Yard. The Yard was one of those places where all the toilet facilities had to be visited a long way from the house, into some old Outhouses where it used to be very cold and dark and needed a lantern. Therefore, we small children were put on bed chamber pots, or what have you, and emptied by Mother accordingly'.*

The family had certainly moved to the Poultry Yard by 1916 as my Father recalls that his younger brother, John, born in September, 1915, was enthralled by seeing Snow for the first time and pestered his mother to let him out of the door (which had a board across to stop him getting out). Father recalls that his mother did no more than pick up John and put him over the board into the snow, which went up to his chest, and he was soon screaming to be picked back out again.

He said his little Brother John also had a *'weak stomach'; certain smells made him sick quickly. He fell over in the poultry yard one day and his hand went into some chicken muck. He put his hand to his nose (as small children do) to smell it and was promptly sick.*

It was also at the bungalow in the Poultry Yard that the accident happened which was to have a profound effect on the rest of my Father's life.

He recalls:

"One day I was wishing to go to the toilet to do my business but being as the earth bog toilet was a long way from the house and it was raining very fast. Mother decided to get one of the crock bedside pots and sit me on that. To my mother's horror the pot shattered to pieces under the right side of my backside,

and it cut my backside quite considerably. I had to be admitted to Moreton Hospital by pony and cart to have first aid and stitching to the wound. I had to stay in hospital for over six to seven weeks. I became a very naughty child to the staff and nurses because I wanted my Mother there with me. The hospital Matron and Sisters stopped Mother visiting me for over six weeks."

His Mother was not allowed by the Nurses to visit him after the first occasion as he cried and played up so much wanting her with him. The consequence was that he did not see her for the rest of his time in Moreton-in-Marsh Hospital. The ward he was in was upstairs at the front.

(This was a time before the National Health Service (NHS) where a Matron was in charge of the running the hospital and set extremely high standards of discipline and cleanliness on the Wards). I think this episode of separation also began to shape my Father's characteristic 'stoicism'.

(Moreton-in-Marsh Cottage Hospital was opened in 1873 at the suggestion of Dr. Leonard Yelf and with the support of Lord Redesdale. The hospital would have been financed by voluntary contributions until taken over by the National Health Service in 1948, and in 1971 was superseded by a newly built hospital in Stow Road. Moreton-in-Marsh). (As of 2021, the old hospital building has been converted into luxury flats and while it was vacant was used as the Police Station in the Father Brown TV Series).

Father said my grandmother received a big bill from Moreton-in-Marsh Hospital for the Surgeons and Doctors' Fees and for his stay of six to seven weeks. *"Mother told me that she would have not been able to pay the said amount. So, I understand Mother who was employed to make butter and provide cream and other produce for the big house (Sezincote House) approached the Head Housekeeper and asked if it would be possible to have an interview with Lady Dugdale. This was granted and as a result 'Lady Dugdale told Mother she would honour the hospital bill for her.'*

(However, while the initial presenting injury was treated, a cut nerve and partly dislocated hip joint was not diagnosed during his admission to the hospital). *"Now mother told me later the amount of damage that had been done to my right hip through the broken crockpot it had cut the nerve system badly and partly dislocated the hip joint from its socket to which was not noticed at the hospital by the people in charge of my care at the time'.* Of course, there were no x-rays at that time. (X rays did not become routine until the 1930's).

This was the beginning of my father's disability which changed his life forever. My Father says *"over the passing years the disability was causing lots of pain and also as I grew the disability was making me limp up and down, quite excessively, which was putting me out of balance quite a lot, as I was only wearing ordinary bought boots of two different sizes because the right foot did not correspond with the left foot in size. This caused him to limp badly as he had a four-inch deficit in his right leg to his left leg.*

Following his discharge from hospital my Grandmother told my Father that they had difficulty in getting him to walk. To strengthen his damaged muscle, he was given a toy horse on wheels with a handle to push around which he called 'Gallithumpian'. *'I was given a four-wheel wooden horse for me to walk and strengthen my legs. I could go very well with him after a while but sometimes he wanted to go faster than me, therefore I used to fall flat on my face when he ran away. So, one day I swore at him. I called him a 'bugger'. On hearing me Mother said 'where the dickens did you learn that from.'* No doubt my Father had heard this expression from the men around the Cowpens and I gather this was not the only name 'Gallithumpian' was given when it fell over taking my Father with it!

My Father was, once he had learned to walk *'and become strong enough'* despite his disability, an adventurous little boy "*When I was able to get about a lot better, I am afraid to say that 'mischief' (or what have you) was being applied in my daily life.*"

I remember one day I was playing with my younger brother just around the corner of the bungalow at the only water supply tap to the house. We had both got going well swilling each other with old tins of water, and also making a lot of mess. All of a sudden due to the noise we were making, around the corner of the house comes Mother to see what was transacted between us. Mother caught me gave me a good slap, because I could not run away fast enough, so Mother took off after my brother she caught him after a short run and slapped him on his bottom, to which he let out a howl and marched him into the house to bed. Then she came back out to look for me, I was hiding behind one of the big fowl roosts keeping an eye on her. When she could not find me, she went back in doors.

When I thought it was safe to move, I ran from my hiding place down into the small wood at the back of the bungalow to emerge on to the footpath leading to the boundary wall of the bungalow, on from there to the stables where I saw Father whom had just come in from the fields, giving his horses a feed and water. He said 'Hello, have you been in mischief, I said 'No'. I stayed with him very close. When he had finished and started off for home, he picked me up and I had a ride on his shoulders.

On arriving up home Mother had got a nice cooked meal for all of us. Of course, on arriving home I was very nervous for fear Mother might tell Father of our misbehaviour of the afternoon, but nothing was disclosed by Mother. I did notice that my brother whom had been reprimanded earlier was also present at the table.

Father also managed to scale the wall *'and run through the small wood at the back of the bungalow down around the front of Sezincote House, up through the big archway out into the big yard, cart sheds and stables. 'I used to sit on the cart shafts and look across at the main kitchens where I knew a friend of Mothers worked as Cook. After a while, when she saw me, a piece of cake or jam tart was forthcoming. After eating that on up the yard I went around the cow pens, had a lick of the stick from the black treacle jar"* (This was a type of molasses which was mixed with the feed of the horses and cows). *"Then on further to the cows and sheep feed bins to have Locust Beans and also I used to fill my small pocket with Sharps meal".* (A type of bran put into the animals feed) *'then make my way 'fully loaded' back home.'* Father was, however, spotted filling his pockets and on arriving back home was relieved of his bountiful food supply by one of the Estate Carters. *'In all the years of my young life did I ever find out how he knew what I had done'.*

As Head Carter on Sezincote Estate my Grandfather was responsible for a team of 12 working horses and Mares in Foal and also keeping working machinery in order. He had two other Carters under his command to supervise and it was a job that took quite an amount of his time and leisure. He was very particular that the horses were well fed for the work that they had to do. The Farm Manager on the Sezincote Estate at the time told him to cut down on the oats he was feeding the horses and reduced the number of sacks he had.

This did not suit my Grandfather. My Father recalls that he went to the 'tallet' (a loft above stalls in a barn where horses are stabled) with my Grandfather and was told to look out for the Farm Manager and to let his Father know when he came. Of course, the inevitable happened and his Father was caught carrying the bags on his shoulder down the stone steps from the tallet. The only thing the Farm Manager said to him was 'that looks heavy, Jack'. (Full Bags of Oats in those days weighed 12 stone). My Father said, '*no more was ever said about cutting down the horses feed*'.

My Father said that my Grandmother would help with the Heavy horses if she was needed to, helping to feed them and take water, but she did not like the thoroughbreds or hunters – they were too flighty and unpredictable.

There was also wood to be had on the Estate for the fire. However, strictly speaking all the trees that fell had to be cut up for the log fires in Sezincote House. After a storm, Grandfather and Shepherd Tidmarsh found that a large beech tree had fallen, in a gulley. Out came the crosscut saw that Grandfather had (which currently I still have in the shed) and the tree was soon cut up and in their woodsheds before the Estate Manager found out about it.

My Father also relates that the coal had to be brought to Sezincote House via the top drive as trades were not allowed to use the bottom drive. This meant that the horses had to pull the coal up the long hill through Bourton on the Hill. The horses had to be kept moving but there was a lady who lived on the hill called Miss Timetts (or some similar name). If the whip was used on the horses, she used to report the Carter to the Sezincote Estate office. Grandfather, however, was very good at 'shacking stones'. If he thought the 'Filler' or any of the other horses, were not 'pulling', he used to 'shack' a small pebble type stone at the horse's backside to remind the horse to pull his weight with the others.

My Father was particularly fond and close to his older sister Lizzie (Annie Elizabeth). One of the Beehive Lodges (on the road to Stow on the Wold from Broadway), caught fire. (The rooves of these lodges used to be thatched. The one, after the fire was tiled, and the other lodge was tiled at a later date when the thatch needed to be renewed).

My Father must have been aged about three at the time. Lizzie wanted to see the 'excitement' because he said she *'dragged him'* as fast as his little legs would go up the drive to the Beehive's. Wood-fellers had been working and he said that he had to scramble over trees that had been felled and evidently wasn't going fast enough for her on his little legs. Exasperated, she evidently picked him up and ran the rest of the way with him. He said '*the thatch was well alight and people were trying to drag whatever furniture they could save outside*'.

LONGBOROUGH SCHOOL

My Father was probably 4 going on 5 when he started at Longborough School. (The School is still in existence as an Infants and Junior School to the present day (2022).

He notes: '*Now as I was between the age of four and a half and five years of age, Mother decided it was time for me to begin school. Therefore, it was arranged that I accompanied my other brothers and sister to the school in Longborough Village.*

His only Sister, Annie Elizabeth, ('*Our Lizzie*') took him to School and they walked along the path from Sezincote Estate. (This path was across the fields and exited by the allotments, the footpath is still there today)

That journey meant me having to walk over a mile each way. Us children had to attend Longborough School as Sezincote Estate happened to be in Longborough Parish. I was together with my brothers and sister at that school until we had to leave Sezincote Estate in 1919 because of a change in circumstances.

It was nice at Longborough School, we had a nice teacher by the name of Miss Gill from Bourton on the Hill Quarry House. Us children whom had to take a packed lunch to eat in the classroom as no other facilities were otherwise available.

In the winter they took a potato to school and the Schoolteacher used to put them in the Fire to bake. *'If it was very cold days, Miss Gill used to tell us to bring a potato, or what have you, so that we could have something warm with our packed lunch (therefore) the kind lady would put the potatoes to bake for us under the grilled fire basket. (Lovely)".* (There were open fires in schools in those days with large guards around them).

"I was lucky some days when I came out of school, the bakers or butchers' employees had just finished delivering to their customers in the Longborough Village or were on their way to Sezincote House and surrounding cottages. They used to stop and pick me up for a ride home. They lifted me up and they used to say 'tell your Mother I will call on her later', and they did."

"There were always small jobs for me to do in the light nights after our cooked meal at around 5.30 to 6.00 p.m. when Father came in. The small jobs like fetching in the logs for Mother, then helping to collect eggs from the four dozen or so fowls laying boxes in the poultry yard and then they were wiped clean. Then helping Mother pack them in boxes. Some for the Sezincote House use and some to be sent to Colonel Dugdale's friends in London and also to other places. A few were also for our own use.

My other Brothers and Sister had to hurry home as they had to change from school clothes into other things and go down to Sezincote House and help get wood blocks and coal into nearly all the main rooms and also help otherwise.

My sister had to assist Mother in the dairy helping to skim the milk and remove the cream. Some had to go in the little containers for the big house use, the rest Mother had to put into the butter making machine to make into butter, again for the big house use, the other to be sent by railway each week to London and elsewhere for Dugdale's friends. All the skimmed milk which was left over was distributed out amongst the Estate employees, those that wanted it, as no charge was made. The employees used to take their cans to be filled by Mother".

(Of course, all the extra help provided through the children was unpaid).

PART 2
CHANGING TIMES

WORLD WAR 1

My Father recalled that his Father did not join up to fight in the war until late in 1917. (My Grandfather's job was classified as agricultural work and as such, technically, he was exempt. However, my Grandfather insisted he was going and enlisted.). (My Father never really knew why my Grandfather decided to join up and Grandmother never spoke about it much to anyone. The truth never came out but it was assumed that a serious row had taken place with the Farm Manager or he may have been influenced by some woodcutters who were working on the Estate at the time) He was *'summoned to Colonel Dugdale's office'* to discuss the conditions of his employment.

"After enlisting and reporting to the depot he was informed that Colonel Dugdale had contacted the army and he was released and was to remain at Sezincote until the harvest had been completed."

Evidently after the harvest *'he was once again summoned to see Colonel and Mrs. Dugdale'* and after ascertaining that my Grandfather was adamant he was still going to war, *'Colonel Dugdale told Father, 'to vacate the house and estate within one month'.* Neither of my Father's older brothers were of an age that they could step into Grandfather's role on the Estate, not even as Under Carters.

(My Grandfather, in 1901, at the age of 17, had boarded with Mark Cook and his family at 1 Upper Terrace in Blockley. Mark, who was born in Bledington, and related by marriage to the family, worked as a Cowman on a farm in Blockley. Grandfather had worked on a local farm (maybe the same one as Mark) as a Carter, so as a consequence he knew the Blockley area quite well).

(My Grandmother and Grandfather walked to Blockley, one Sunday in 1917, They met young Morris Eastbury and he told them that Chesher the Miller had one of the cottages empty at the top of Mill Lane (we always called it Chesher's Lane, but it was also known as Hobbs Lane and Watery Lane)

'My Father and Mother left us (likely my Father and his younger brother John, as the other two boys, William and George were older)) *with my Sister and we were told 'to behave and go to bed promptly'. We did not see Father and Mother return from their house hunting journey that night but the next morning we were told that we would be moving to Blockley as they had managed to find one of the empty properties available to move into'.*

'None of the children nor their Mother wanted to leave Sezincote Estate but we had to' During the procedure of packing up of the few items which we possessed all had to help.

The day came that we had to find someone who would oblige with transport to come and move us from Sezincote, lock stock and our few belongings. In desperation Mother took it upon herself to approach both of the Dugdales to ask if they would be kind enough to supply transport of some kind for us to move. To Mother's surprise, Mother's request was refused. It was explained to Mother that employers only helped new labour move from their old employment to their new jobs and not away from their old employment.

More by luck than judgement, Mother mentioned our circumstances to one of the Under Carters (the one who used to take the Sharps out of my pockets most days) about our situation and he told Mam that he knew a man in Blockley by the name of Jim Webb who owned two horses and trolley and told her to go and see him at the wood end of Blockley. Mother and our two oldest boys walked down one evening (leaving John and me in charge of big Sister Lizzie) and managed to find Jim Webb. He volunteered to come and move us, but it would have to be on a Sunday, as he had a contract with the Council hauling stone and other items. A Sunday was arranged for moving in the latter part of May 1917.

When the horses and trolley arrived, Mr. Webb said he had to apply for permission to enter Sezincote Estate. Therefore. it did not take us long to load our few bits and sticks and make our way to our new abode in the village of Blockley.

MOVING HOME

My Father relates that the weather the day they moved into the house at Chesher's Lane was awful, very wet and cold. *It must have been one of our unlucky days, as it was pouring with rain from start to finish. Nearly everyone was wet through. My Brother John was in the pram covered up. Myself and Sister were sat on back of the trolley covered over with sheets. My other two brothers and Mother who walked from Sezincote Estate to Blockley were very wet indeed.*

The horse and trolley they hired to carry what little furniture they had could not pull it up Chesher's Lane and they had to unload it at the bottom and carry it up to the house.

After unloading we soon had a fire going and Mother mustered up some food to eat. 'Bill Hooper (his family lived next door) gave us enough sticks to light a fire and a bucket of coal'. The work started getting all things a bit shipshape. Mother managed to get things in order very quickly as well, such as bakers, groceries, etc.

My Father remembers the house they came from at Sezincote as comfortable and warm, in contrast to the house at the top of Chesher's Lane which was cold and in poor repair. The family also suffered the loss of access to the eggs, milk and butter, pig, rabbits and potatoes that had been available to them at Sezincote. (The Sezincote Estate allowed its workers to plant a long row of potatoes in a field each year). Also. when they were at Tuckwell's Lodge, before they moved into the Poultry Yard, they had been eligible for a ton of coal from Bourton on the Hill Parish Relief and although they lost this when they moved to the Poultry Yard, there was plenty of fire-wood accessible on the Estate for the Workers. The disadvantage of moving to the Poultry Yard had been the loss of one of the visiting grocers, as at Tuckwells Lodge both Horne's and Drury's from Moreton-in-Marsh, had called but when they moved to the Poultry yard, Dugdale's would not allow two grocers on the Estate proper, so only one of the Grocers was able to call.

The rent for the house at Blockley was 3s.6d. per week – a lot of money in those days. I am sure Grandfather would have arranged for his army pay to be sent home, but I have no doubt that the years between 1918 and 1920 when my Grandfather returned home, were particularly uncomfortable for my Father. They lived in this house up to 1928 when they bought and moved into Pitt Cottage. My Father also relates that Old Chesher also wanted to put the rent up to 4s.6d. a week but the women stood their ground and told him that until he mended the roof, they were not going to pay any more.

The roof of the house leaked. Father recalls that they moved the old beds around the bedroom under the untorched roof (through which you could see the stars) and when it rained also moved the 'guzunder's and buckets, strategically round the room to catch the water from the leaks. They also had great coats as bedcovers. *"You could lay in bed and see stars and moon through the roof in the garret". Their bedroom overlooked Chesher's Lane and the window overlooking the lane can just be seen in the photograph below:*

Picture just shows houses at top of Mill Lane jutting into High Street.

My Father relates that one night the floor gave way under one of the legs of the bed, tipping him and his brother John out of bed. This could have been quite serious, as, had the floor given way, they would have fallen through 2 floors down the stairwell.

Facilities were shared between the three cottages. There was one earth closet for 3 families and one copper for washing clothes shared by those families. Their neighbours were the Stanley Family and the Hooper Family.

My Father often related the story that when Clare (Stanley) used to be given an orange she used to get into the toilet and stay there until she had finished eating it to avoid sharing it with her siblings. Father said that, *'if you wanted to use the toilet it didn't matter what you did to try and prise her out of there – (even pour water through the leaky roof), she just would not budge'.* In the end, if they were desperate, they had to go under the Horse Chestnut tree at the back of Rouse's garage or *'up the fields'*. (Clare Stanley was to become a teacher in Blockey School in later years).

My Father said that his Mother was always the one who started the 'copper' on Mondays, (the traditional washing day). The other Mothers would then use the water after Grandmother had done her washing. Father said that the Stanley's used to hang their knickers over the gooseberry bushes to dry and that there were *'more holes than knicker'.*

FATHER RETURNS

John (always called 'Jack') Hicks, my Grandfather did not return from WW1 until 1920. He had been badly wounded in his neck and right shoulder and was never able to use the arm properly again. After returning to England, initially to Netley in Southampton, he was then transferred to a hospital in Dundee and then to another Hospital in Birmingham. While in hospital he made several embroideries and a Vicar's Easter Stole. The Quartermaster in Dundee gave him a Book of Pictures of Dundee which is signed by the Quartermaster. All my Grandfather's memorabilia have been accepted and sent to the Imperial War Museum.

My Father told me that when my Grandfather was discharged from the hospital in Birmingham on the way home he bought a Pony and walked back with it. The family called it 'Our Jimmy' My Father and Grandfather did a lot of work with 'Jimmy and the Trolley'.

Grandfather at the bottom of School Lane with 'our Jimmy' (Chesher's Mill in background).

FAMILY PETS

Although my Grandparents always reared pigs and chickens and sometimes rabbits for the table, they also had a dog and three cats (not all at once).

The Dog was called Rover, I do not know the exact circumstances that they acquired him, but would speculate that it may have been from my Grandfather's Brother, Albert Edward, who by that time, I believe was employed as a Shepherd near Oxford. Rover was an old English Sheepdog and was still alive when my Mother met my Father in the 1940's as she used to take 'Old Rover' for walks when she came to Blockley and also spoke about him very affectionately to me. During WW2 Rover was also able to identify the planes that flew over or near Pitt Cottage by their sound. He only barked and growled at the noise German Planes made while residing under the round dining table in my Grandmother's Living Room.

My Grandmother first cat, brought home (like the others) from the Brickworks as kittens in my Father's Dinner bag, grew into a very large ginger tom cat called George. George was good at catching half-grown rabbits in the field opposite Pitt Cottage. One day Les Webb (the Webbs lived near the Dovedale further up the street), mistook him for a rabbit and shot at him. George made it home and Grandmother found him bleeding in the old wash house minus his ear. My Grandfather and Grandmother were extremely cross about this, but fortunately, George recovered and lived to catch more rabbits.

Tibbers was the second cat to arrive. Tibbers was my Father's favourite and she kept him company in bed at night. There was a large pile of wood stacked at the front of the cottage for a while and it made it very easy for Tibbers to access the bedroom where my Father slept (the one nearest Middle Cottage). Tibbers used to climb up the wood pile and present my Father with live mice she had caught. She dumped them on or in the bed and Father had to scrabble to catch them and put them out again. Tibbers was still alive when I was a child in the 1950's and was a lovely long haired fluffy cat that I absolutely adored and she obviously forgave my childhood 'handlings' and never scratched me.. She had a favourite place to curl up on, on my Grandmother's Chaise Lounge. Over the years a round depression had appeared where she constantly curled up and it was there until I was absolutely forced to get the Chaise reupholstered around 2013. I was really sad to see the 'dunt' she had made go.

Benjamin was the last cat to come into the household. He grew into a large tabby cat. He also scratched me on the face. It was my own fault because I was trying to grab him from under Grandmother's round table. (I had been warned by Grandmother and Mother not to do this). He was not as tolerant as Tibbers, so went for me. I was a really nasty child and remember bawling and saying 'Put him in the frying pan, put him in the fire'. I am appalled now I am older that I said that. However, Grandmother and Mother pacified me and I forgave him as it was my fault. I was however, careful not to annoy him in the future.

VILLAGE LIFE

The transition to life in the village of Blockley and the loss of the personal freedom of wandering round a big Estate like Sezincote, was a difficult one for a little boy of about 6 years old.

At Longborough Church of England School my Father had his big Sister 'Lizzie' to 'look out for him'. Born in July, 1907, she was already ten years old by the time my Father started at Longborough School at around the age of 5. She was evidently a strong girl as getting to the fire at the Beehive Lodges she had *'picked him up and run with him'*.

However, when my Father started to attend Blockley Church of England Girls and Infants School, in 1919, she was 12 years old and by the age of 13 had left that school to start work as a servant at Wellacres Farm. (This was a position my Grandparents removed her from as she was being asked not only to carry out work in the house but also to work on the farm and my Grandparents felt this was far too onerous for her). She then obtained a position as a servant to Countess Pollitt who lived at The Silk Mill in Sleepy Hollow, Blockley. In this position she also travelled to London with Countess Pollitt and looked after her pug dogs when the Countess did not take them with her.

At the age of 7, the boys from Blockley, Church of England, Girls and Infants School were transferred to 'the big boys' school in Park Road.

My Father, thus had to *'stand up for himself'*, when he went to the Boys School and as a little boy with a disability was forced to prove that he was as strong as the other boys.

My Father writes:

"Now that I, together with my family have moved into a cottage in Blockley from Sezincote, I found my life must go on with a difference in many ways.

After coming to Blockley and attending school there, it was very funny for quite a while for me because when I was at Longborough School we used to have to take some sandwiches but when I started at the Blockley School it was Mother who suggested that I came home to lunch of what was available at the time, a nice sandwich or if cold a nice bowl of home-made soup. At night when we were all present at the table there was always a nice cooked meal and plenty of it."

He goes on to say:

So, firstly about a week or so after arriving in the village, on a Monday morning, I was taken by my Mother to the local Junior School (Church of England, Blockley Girls and Infants School in New Lane now called School Lane), whereupon, I was introduced to the Head Teacher's pupils. I had to attend the junior school of mixed girls and boys because I was not yet seven years of age. It was only after seven years of age that boys and girls went their separate ways. I was in the junior side of the school for about 8 to 9 months. Then transferred to the higher section in the School. My word what a difference. It was in that section under the Head Teacher, Mrs. Bennett, instead of the teacher I started under, Miss Collett.

Now I remember quite well one morning, the Head Teacher said "now you boys and girls, I would like to re-organise the class a little as is customary in most junior mixed schools with children of your ages. I would like a boy and girl to sit together" which she done after playtime one morning. Well, that seemed to work very well.

Father showed his caring side for his classmates by recording an incident in one of the classes he attended. He was used to cleaning up at home so didn't hesitate to help his friend.

Now, it was made compulsory if either a boy or girl needed to use the toilet we each were obliged to put up our hands and ask teacher if we could. Now it came about in this case that the nice little girl that was sitting next to me put up her hand several times but the teacher did not seem to notice of her wishes to go to the toilet. Therefore, this poor little girl all of a sudden started to wet her little buttoned up knickers and the little girl was becoming very agitated when she saw the wet running over the floor. Therefore, me just thinking of the poor girl's predicament I jumped up quickly and ran out to the cloakroom to find a cloth (to which I was taught at home) to wipe up the wet off the floor. Ho, when the Teacher noted what was going on, my word did she tell me off good and proper. Then she saw the predicament this little girl was in. She pulled her out of the desk, crying and took her out to the cloakroom and cleaned her up. The teacher must have found some other dry knickers from somewhere because the girl had something wrapped up in paper in her hand on return to our desk. Oh, my word, her little face was flushed, therefore, she tried very hard to hide her misfortune but my calm ways soon put a smile back on her face after talking to her nicely. Quite a few years later until she left the village, I used to be given a nice hello and a smile should we meet up.

SENIOR SCHOOL, BLOCKLEY

Now after the Christmas holiday recess of the year 1919, I together with several other boys were removed from the Junior School in School Lane up to the Senior Boys in Park Road as we had reached the age of 7 years, which seemed to make us grown up. The School of Boys were taught by nearly all men – except Miss Gallagher and Miss Dee.

My Father, 2nd from Left, Second Row

My Father's first teacher at the Church of England, Blockley Boys School was the aforesaid, Miss Dee. However, it soon became obvious to my Father that the expectations of the Headmaster at the time varied depending on the social status of the pupil. Some, boys, (those whose parents could afford the expense of sending their child to the Grammar School) were expected to go on to the Grammar School at Chipping Campden, the others were expected to go no further than find themselves some sort of work. This led to a variable level of teaching and my Father firmly felt that his last year there was wasted because of the attitude of the headmaster. Apparently, the bigger boys who weren't designated to go to the Grammar School were used to cut and carry turf from Charlie Dee's Farm, Park Farm on the road to Bourton on the Hill from the Easter until the boys left at the beginning of Summer. This turf was used to create a lawn area at the School.

My Father writes: *'After I have been in the village for some time and attending school, things seemed to be getting itself into a better situation by making new friends and rebelling against others, therefore I had to learn to stand up for myself somewhat, even if I was permanently disabled. There were quite a lot of fisty cuffs transacted sometimes before it was realized that I was as strong as some others.*

As some of us bigger boys began to show some strength and authority in the part of the village I lived in, it resulted that we had got some of the boys that we did not want on our patch of ground running home and telling their mothers of our behaviour towards them. The Hicks and Gills and the Hales, were my Father's little 'gang' etc. *The boy's Mothers used to come down the street and shout their abuse and also sometimes they would complain to Mother concerning our roughness towards them. Mother used to tell the boy's Mothers that "your boys must learn to stick up for themselves like my boys have".*

From my Father's notes of this time, there is no doubt that his 'little gang' got up to a lot of mischief. My Father uses the term 'roughnecks' throughout the narrative and storytelling of this time to describe the group of boys 'in his gang' and who also took part in many escapades with him. Some of these 'escapades' I have included in a separate chapter at the end of the book as they reflect some of the mischief that adolescent boys aged between 12 and 14 'got up to' in the village. Some of this cannot be termed as 'mischief' because, although skipping school, they were performing a useful social purpose, such as helping to pump the manual Village Fire Engine that attended some serious fires in the village in my Father's youth.

'Skipping' or 'truancy' from School, whatever the reason, was treated in the same way, with corporal punishment. Quite often the Headmaster asked the Vicar what punishment should be meted out and invariably it was 'the cane'. The Rev. Ager was the Rector of Blockley between 1919 and 1929.

This is not to say that my Father did not have enough to occupy his time, as my Grandmother and Grandfather expected the boys to help with the garden, pigs and chickens they kept on The Warren, by carrying up food and water and cleaning out henhouses and pigsties.

School Holidays

'As each school holiday came around, we would try and find jobs to do. We would make inquiries to find out if any of the farmers or any business people needed jobs done so that we could earn a few pennies for our own pockets. It was no use asking Mother for pennies as she needed all she could get to buy food and clothes for the family.

Sometimes I was lucky and helped a farmer with his haymaking or threshing, such as bond cutting on the drum, or any other transaction that brought a penny or two into my pocket. Should there not be a job about and you were under Mother's feet she would say 'get up on the Warren and clean the fowls or pigs out", or chop and saw wood for the fire lighting in the morning, one was not allowed to hang about doing nothing as you were relying on them for your food and clothes.

It was only in the final two years at the Senior School that my Father's struggle with his disability began to be noticed as he was unable, but not unwilling, to take part in the PT lessons. However, before this happened, the arrival of two young female teachers caused some excitement among these adolescent boys.

My Father writes:

'Now one day a big surprise came about. One morning the Head Teacher came into our classroom and introduced us boys to two young female students which were just starting out into their teaching professions. The teacher said 'one of the young students will be taking you boys in PT exercises. The other will act as an under teacher helping pupils whom needed help'. Now, my word, after the teacher had left our class the commotion and thoughts that went through us old rough necks minds was tremendous. It

was not long before help was needed with the requests that were asked for, I can tell you. Now I won't dwell upon this subject too much, but I will relate about only one of the subjects that did happen accidentally one morning. The boys in the desk in front of my friends and mine, asked for attention from the young pupil teacher. I'm sorry to say that due to the distraction that was caused when the pupil teacher suddenly bent over to attend to that boy's needs there happened to be quite a few pens and pencils dropped onto the floor. Do you know it happened that quite a few of my friends and mine sums were marked wrong, after that. *Now as regards the girl PT student she was working under the instructions of the Head Teacher. She was only to take one class in the morning and one in the afternoon for half hour sessions. I am afraid we only had the PT student at our school for about 12 months because she had to go to a bigger school up London way. So, we had to receive our PT through one of the other teachers when time allowed"* (PT 'physical training' now called PE 'physical education')

RECOGNITION OF AND HELP FOR MY FATHER'S DISABILITY

My Father writes:

I was practically in my last year at School and growing fast and finding that due to the shortness of my right leg to the length of my left, I found that the limp between left and right legs was getting worse and causing quite a lot of inconvenience to me particularly doing jobs etc., and also out in the playground on exercise. I had complained to the PT teacher that I could not fully do all the exercises that was required of me to do. Therefore, he spoke to the school boss and it was decided between the PT Teacher and the school that I could stop in class and read books whilst the PT Teacher took the rest of the class in exercise. It only lasted a few weeks when all of a sudden one morning when the class was out in the playground on exercise that the school boss came into my classroom, which was a shock, where I was sitting and reading and said 'Hello Hicks'. I said 'Good Morning Sir'. He then sat down on the desk and referred to me of my disability and also what I thought I was capable of doing such as exercise, etc., the inconvenience it must be causing me. So, after thought, I said, 'yes, it was very inconvenient' Then after a while he said 'I will see what can be done for you in life'. Then this school boss said that the school medical doctor, whom you have met before, and his staff are due at the school in about one to two weeks. I will see that you will have an interview with him and his staff advisors. I said 'thank you'. So, it was left at that.

Now this is what happened to me about 9/10 days later. One morning just before the 12 o'clock lunch break, the Head Master comes into the classroom where I was and gave the under teacher some green cards which meant, either his nurse head hunter of lice or the medical Doctor was coming soon to inspect the boys whom the cards were for. Now it came about that the school boss was true to his word and that my name was on one of those cards.

I was given a card to give to Mother or Father whom could be with me to attend the medical. Now of course it had to be Mother to attend.

When the day arrived for the meeting and my turn came round and my name was called to the room. I goes to be greeted by the Medical Doctor and also the local village nursing sister also two more medical associates and of course Mother. Then medical doctor started saying 'we hope we are going to decide what is best suited to help your disability'. The Doctor told me to sit down. Then the Doctor, his staff, the nurse and of course Mother went into a separate part of the class room, they all sat down with the Doctor and had a long discussion.

The Doctor came and said he would like some measurements of my height and also how high my right foot was up off the ground when I stood upright on left foot which was found turned out to be about 1 and a half inches of space that the Doctor said I was having to limp up and down each step and therefore it needed some sort of support raising to the boot to level me up.

Now, when the medical was over between Doctor and other medical staff and also Nurses and of course Mother, it was *agreed that the Doctor write out and give a medical certificate to Mother that Mother* could take to *the local Village Shoe and Boot Repairer, a Mr. Ledbetter. When we arrived at Mr. Ledbetter's workshop in Mount Pleasant, Blockley, not far from School, he asked what we required so Mother gave him the Doctors certificate and after studying it for a few minutes he then said to me, 'stand up in that chair will you', he then started to take measurements, he also put different sizes of wood blocks under my right foot. He then measured the height it needed between the chair and my right foot to bring me up level with the left foot. After a lot of measurements and etc., were complete., Mr. Ledbetter discussed the situation with Mother. Then he said he thinks he could make a raise to the heel of a boot, but not the right sole because he thought it was not needed at this time of making operations. He said it would take him two to three weeks.*

After about two weeks Mr Ledbetter sent for me to carry out a rough fitting. which turned out perfectly, and Mr. Ledbetter was very pleased. He told me to come back in about 3 to 4 days. My Father notes that 'when I was able to collect the boot and show him how I could walk with it, I nearly fell over at first but I very soon got used to it and enjoyed it very much.' The boot that was made by Mr. Ledbetter had a raised heel of about one and half inches, and my Father notes: *Now with that boot job accomplished I was able to move about somewhat better, such as walking and running and I also found that more odd jobs could be done by me for pocket money'.*

My Father goes on to say, that his Mother was firmly told that it would be the last school medical test concerning my disability. *'Therefore, should I need further alterations to my boot, I, or my parents would have to arrange things themselves with Mr. Ledbetter.'*

The boot lasted my Father until he left school and was about to find employment (about two years). It was noticed by his Father and Mother that *'I was limping more again and therefore needed some more raising to the right boot (as I was growing pretty fast). Dad approached Mr. Ledbetter again to see if he would make another bigger boot. Mr. Ledbetter said to Dad that 'he was not qualified to make a proper surgical boot fit enough for me to go to work with, but he did recommend a proper surgical appliance maker who was at Mr. Wheatley's shop in High Street, Evesham.*

Mother wrote to the shop and received notification of a convenient day to visit the shop. Father and Mother took me to Evesham and asked the assistant if it was possible for them to see the surgical boot makers. I was ushered into the workshop and after Father stated my case measurements were taken and other particulars. After that was done the surgical man said he would notify us again in two months. I found employment at Butlers timber yard at Draycott within those two months and one day a card came by post to say a fitting of the boot was ready and could I together with my parents attend on the date on the card. We went to the shop and after the fitting it came as quite a big surprise for Father and Mother because the surgical man said 'when the boot was finished and ready for collection it would cost them in the region of about £6.00. I am sorry to say both Mother and Father nearly fell through the floor, they were also told the boot would have to last 2 to 3 years at least because of the making expense. Therefore, I am glad to say it did, together with a few minor repairs necessary from time to time.

When it came about that after 3 years I needed some more raising to my right boot (or a new one) Father said we would go to the surgical man at Wheatleys in Evesham to make further arrangements and get advice concerning further improvements to the boot. When we asked to see the surgical man to our surprise we were told he had retired and also Wheatleys had finished dealing with surgical boots and shoes. Father asked if any other place existed in Evesham but the Senior Assistant said. No, but they recommended 'Salt's in the Bull Ring in Birmingham.

After we returned home and discussed the situation it was decided to venture down to Birmingham and find M. Salt's Shop. (Dad had some idea where it was). We found the shop and were interviewed by an oldish assistant who introduced us to the surgical boot man. The surgical man took over and started by asking about the other boots made and then he turned to me and looked me up and down then said 'take your big boot off' and looked at it and after his inspection of the boot his reply was 'Yes, I will make him a boot to his requirements'. Out came his measuring rest of blocks, tape measures and so forth, so again after lots of measurements with tape and blocks, he said, 'that's fine. I will notify your parents in due course in about 2 months'. We then left for home.

After a wait of about 8 to 9 weeks we were notified that the boot was ready and could be collected. Also, in the notification was an outline of the bill with the stated price of around £12 to £14.00.

That boot lasted 4 years until I had to go through the same procedure again.

When the boot had to be replaced in the 1940's my Father had already met Doris (always called Dora) Moore at a dance at Moreton-in-Marsh Aerodrome. Dora was working as an Assistant Store Manager at the NAAFI.

On the penultimate visit to get a new boot, my Father was able to take Dora with him as she was able to get a day off work. My Father writes as follows: *'Now as regards the third surgical boot I had to have made by Salts of Birmingham. The day I received the card from Salts it stated that they were not dealing with surgical people on Saturdays any longer as it was detrimental to their business. They wrote and said any other day of the week I could visit their shop and see the surgical bootmaker. That put me in a bit of a quandry as it meant my losing a day off work and also Mam and Dad said they would not be able to go this time.*

In the end things turned out very well as I was great friends with Mr. and Mrs. Hodgkins of the Royal Oak Public House in the village. Therefore, one Friday night when I was helping assist Mrs. Hodgkins with serving the customers I happened to mention my predicament to her after closing time. about the journey to Salts at Birmingham.

'Ha, she said , 'I know where they are. I will accompany you there when you have to go', therefore I thanked her and told her the date. Then Mrs. Hodgkins said 'why not make it a threesome as it was also the same time that I was courting Dora Moore, my girl friend whom Mrs. Hodgkins had met several times. Mrs. Hodgkins then said if Dora could get a day off work we could make a third party. So, by luck. that was arranged and Dad fetched Dora over the night before we went. So, the day of the interviews came and off we went down on the train and Mrs. Hodgkins knew just where to go to the shops. Then when all the paraphanalia was transacted Mrs. Hodgkins said we will catch so and so No bus and go and visit some very close friends of hers and we went with her for the rest of the day. So that's what we done and had a good time.

We returned home on the train and was escorted from the Station on the last of Mr. Rouses train meeting bus of the day.

Now when the days of waiting to hear for notification that the boot was ready for collection, I said to Mrs. Hodgkins that Mam and Dad could not accompany me again to Salts for collection of the boot. Mrs. Hodgkins said she would accompany me again but alas only the two of us this time, as Dora could not get time off. So, on the day stated on the card off we went before dawn to the station on the bus and train to Birmingham and to Salts to collect boots and pay £14.00. I was told the boot would have to last another 4 years and so it did I am glad to say. To fill the day Mrs. Hodgkins and me visited her friends again and enjoyed ourselves, then returned as before.

It was late in 1945 that I collected that last boot from Salts and was told the length of time it had to last (4 years).

In 1947, and after his marriage to Dora, on 3lst May, 1947 my Father began to have problems with his right leg and was in some pain and had difficulty getting out of bed. Dr. Jean Haine (one of the local Doctors who lived in Blockley, Dr. Jean and her husband Dr. Frank Haines who lived at Box Cottage) was called to look at my Father and he was told that she was going to send him to the Wingfield Hospital in Oxford for further inspection by a Surgeon.

On 8th June, 1933, my Father purchased his a bicycle from J. Gardner, Ironmonger, Blockley, (now a house called Church Gates). A copy of the receipt is undernoted.

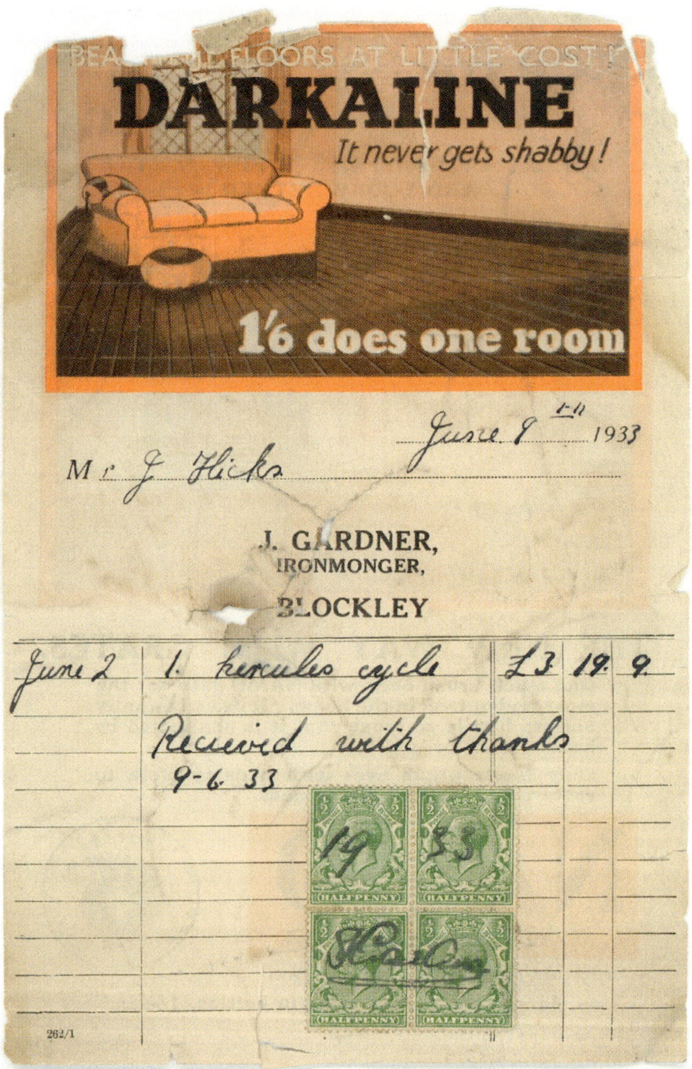

My Father rode this bicycle until the operation on his hip at the Wingfield Hospital late in 1948. The operation fused a bone from the shin of his good leg into the hip of his right leg, and was performed by Professor Foley. However, as a result of this operation my Father was no longer able to pedal the cycle. This meant that for many years, until the early 1960's when he passed his driving test and bought a 3 wheeled Bond Motor car from the Motor House at Stoulton (on the road from Evesham to Worcester), (he had the Bond fitted with hand controls), he walked over a mile to work and back and while he was at work walked to the Pumping Station, situated in front of the mansion and to the Reservoir below the wood called Augustus several times a day; wheeled barrows-full of coke around the camp and to the bunkers inside the big boiler house where he was also one of the stokers of the 3 Robin Hood Major Boilers that kept the camp supplied with hot water, (as well as maintaining the Pumping Station and Reservoir) at the then NAB Polish Hostel on the site of the American Army Hospital at Northwick Park. He did this until it closed and he was transferred to the Fire Service College at Moreton-in-Marsh in the 1970's.

At the Fire College his job was setting up the instruments for fire monitoring equipment, maintaining and mending small electrical appliances and general maintenance on the site.

I remember this bicycle, as it was hanging up in a shed at the Mill when I was small. It was never used again after his operation in 1948. I assume that when they moved from 6 Mill Row to my Grandparent's house at Pitt Cottage, my Father disposed of the cycle then as he did most of their household furniture, much to my Mother's consternation.

REFLECTIONS ON THE FAMILY MOVE TO BLOCKLEY

I have often thought that had the family stayed at Sezincote and not moved into Blockley in 1919, when my Father was six years old, my Father may not have gained mechanical skills that stood him in good stead throughout his life and may have, like his older brothers, remained tied into agricultural employment. In those days a lot of young men joined one of the Forces because of lack of work in the Villages at the time. However, because of his disability, that option would not have been open to my Father.

The house the family moved into at the top of Chesher's Lane (Mill Lane) was opposite Rouse' Garage. (Before the First World War and shortly after, Rouse's ran horse drawn transport. Goods and people were transported to and from Blockley Station. They also hired a horse and brougham for general travel and provided the hearse for the village. (The hearse was kept at what is now the Coach House below Rock Cottage and the horses that pulled the hearse and the brougham were stabled at what is now Chapel Cottage opposite). My Father told me the horses names: there was Gypsy and her foal, a gelding they were both black with a white blaze and a matched pair that used to pull the Hearse. Then there was Gunner an old grey War Horse with his army number branded on his hip (one of the 60,000 lucky younger horses returned from WW1 and sold to farmers or hauliers) and also Ginger, a Chestnut, that pulled the Brougham).

Not long after the First World War Rouse's became, in my Father's words 'mechanised'. They bought a bus and also the first Model T Ford into the village. A travelling mechanic called Bertie Ford worked for them. (He had been in the Royal Air Corp during WW1, which became the Royal Air Force in 1918) and this was the man, who sensing an interested little boy, taught my Father all about engines. By the age of 12, my Father could strip down the engine of a Model T Ford, help to regrind the valves and put it back together again.

'When I was between the age of 10 to 14 years, we lived close to Mr. Rouse's garage. I used to help the garage owner and their travelling mechanic with car repair jobs (all for pocket money) on cars, buses, or what have you. When out on running in trials with the vehicles which had been repaired the mechanic used to let me take the steering wheel sometimes and by him doing that I learnt to drive very well before my 14th birthday.

I served car and motorcycle customers with petrol and oil, also washed cars and put wind in their car tyres and nearly everything else in general concerning cars. (In those days petrol and oil came in drums and had to be pumped out of the drums into the tanks of the cars and lorries).

Grace Rouse, George Rouse's daughter used to drive the Model T Ford. If the village Doctor was called out at night my Father had to go with her, because, while she could drive the vehicle, she could not 'swing' the engine to start it, but my Father, as a strong young boy, (despite his disability), could.

One night the Doctor was called out to a house on the Springhill Estate to a confinement. It was during the winter and very snowy. They were at the cottage there for a long time and by the time they started back, more snow had fallen. My Father recalled, encouraging and instructing Grace to weave the car from side to side to get up the hill (Kennel Hill) out of The Dingles and back up on to the Stow Road.

Because of his disability there must have been some concern about my Father's suitability for employment, however, he notes: *'As I attained the age of 14 years in the October and left school my next problem or that of my parents was to seek some sort of employment for me of some description (like today, trades were not learnt at school) and beggars could not be choosers'.*

While my Father was waiting to find a job, he helped the family by feeding the pigs and fowls and digging the garden ground they rented on The Warren. *'After I had been left school a considerable time, one day I was most fortunate in one respect that I happened to be on very friendly terms with George Sharpe's son who was working at the local sawmills at Draycott. (Dennis Sharpe)'.* (Dennis and George Rouse, my Grandfather, Jack Hicks and others used to accumulate round the garage, Rouses Garage, on the corner of Chesher's Lane) and stand and talk.)

(My Grandfather had been severely wounded in WW1 and did not return home until 1920 having been in various hospitals, Netley in Southampton and Dundee and was discharged from a hospital in Birmingham.

He was unable to return to his old job as the Head Carter on Sezincote Estate and to fill in time and to earn a little money drove the cars occasionally for Rouses until the Dyer brothers took him on in 1924 when they were contracted by Captain Churchill to clear and level the oversite on which to build the, then, new brickworks, Northwick Brick and Tile Works Limited near Blockley Station).

My Father goes on to say: 'The Sharpe family were related by marriage to the Rouse family. *One night when he came home Dennis Sharpe ('Old Shaver' was his nickname) asked Father if he could approach the owner of the sawmill* (Jack Butler) *for me concerning a job. Father said 'yes please' with the result* that Shaver came round that night and said 'your boy can start at the Timber Yard sawdust carrying and then can go on the 'push up' bench with Jackie Hopes. So, *I was given employment working on one of the saw benches together with the Head Sawyer,* the said, Jackie Hopes. *I am pleased to say my progress at that job was fast with the result* that Shaver wanted a mate for the Lorry and I went on that and another kid from Draycott got the job on the 'push up' bench. The lorry was *one of the travelling motorised timber waggons which brought trees into the sawmill from all over the Cotswold district and beyond.*

Butlers were Timber Merchants from Birmingham. It was Charles Butler who lived in Draycott. I believe they may also have had Plantations abroad because my Father said that Charles Butler travelled abroad a lot.

A lot of the trade that Butler's did was in Elm 'Coffin Boards' and these were loaded on the trains at Blockley Station probably to go to London.

At the time, Butler's were not only felling trees all around Blockley, Draycott and land they owned at Paxford but also at Sherbourne Park between Burford and Northleach. Big timber carriages drawn by Heavy Horses carried the logs back to the Timber Yard at Draycott. However, the timber yard also had motorised timber waggons and it was on one of these that my Father acted as 'Shavers' mate.

My Father remembers travelling with Dennis Sharpe 'Shaver' in the lorry to Sherbourne Park and on the way back they had to stop on the road between Bourton on the Water and Stow on the Wold (along by the Barn halfway along the road on the left after what is now Guilder's Transport 2022), to fill up with water from a ditch because the lorry had started to boil because of the heavy load they were carrying.

My Father goes on to say: '*On reaching my 16th birthday and only able to earn 12 shillings per week at that job, I decided to ask Mr. Butler's son, Jack, for more wages. I did just that, only to be told the job did not warrant any more. So, to earn more I was given an alternative. I could go and live in a caravan and work with the sawyers whom operated the portable sawing apparatus. This consisted of one rack saw bench and one push up saw bench and a water carrier. If I joined them, I would live away from home from Monday morning until Friday night and I would be paid the wage of 16 shillings per week (quite a sum of money in those days).*

I talked the subject over with Father and Mother and decided to join the gang as work was very scarce in Blockley at the time. I informed my employer that I had decided to join the portable gang of sawyers and asked what my duties would consist of. His reply to that question was, the job to be done would consist of my keeping the portable steam engine supplied with water, which had to be pumped and carted with a horse drawn water carrier from the nearest brook which was in the region of a mile from the engine and sawing base. So, one Monday morning in 1927, I cycled together with the other employees of the sawing gang from Blockley via Broadway to New Town Cross Roads on the Cheltenham Road where we turned right past the Hobnails Public House, to the next turn left which went to Gotherington Village where the portable sawing equipment was based.

My Father was sent with the gang of Tree fellers to Gotherington Fields, to fell the Oaks and probably Elms on Dixton Hill, which you can see as you face towards Cheltenham from the Hob Nail's Public House on the road to Tewkesbury before the Evesham to Cheltenham main road (A46).

They all lived in a Caravan (more a Shepherd's Hut) and Father was responsible for fetching and carrying water for the steam engine with a horse and a small tank; peeling potatoes, preparing the meal, walking to get milk from the Innkeeper at the Hobnails at 5.30 in the morning – straight from the cow (he often had to wait for the Innkeeper to finish milking the cow) and various other jobs that the tree-fellers might require. Father is the little one on the left in the photograph (below) in the short trousers and the hat. The steam engine is shown behind.

The work was very hard and living conditions far from good and I was only too pleased when Friday night came around so that I could cycle back home to Blockley and get my feet under Mother's table again and get stuck into a square cooked meal.

Some weekends my Father had to ride one of the Heavy Shire Horses from Dixton Hill all the way to Butler's Timber yard at Draycott and on Monday morning he rode the Heavy Horse back to Dixton Hill. He never had any trouble with the horses. He had a bag thrown over their back to sit on.

At the sawing base I was living and sleeping in a big caravan which slept twelve and sometimes fourteen workmates at times, therefore the atmosphere was a bit thick. I was up in the mornings by six o clock, and outside into the cold morning air to wash and answer the call of nature out under the hedge! Then it was back to breakfast and get whatever you had got in your locker because we had to take all the food we needed for the week, with the exception of bread, as one could buy loaves from a baker as he passed by the gate where we worked. The Portable engine driver and working foreman used to do a bit of black-market bargaining with the old farmer who owned the ground who let us have a rabbit or two and some eggs and milk in exchange for loads of sawn logs and sawdust for his cowpens. I was on that job until nearly Christmas of that year and it was starting to get very cold indeed. I was having to put my feet and legs down into my pullover sleeves when I was in bed at night to help me keep warm. I was beginning to take a dislike to the job and conditions and I happened to mention the predicament I was in one weekend to my Father and Mother. They were up in arms immediately so after some careful

thought between them and me, it was decided I went straight down to my employers Draycott Office to hand in my notice because of the conditions. It was accepted, I must say with some remorse, after he had tried further bargaining concerning better conditions, but *he found it was to no avail.*

The work at Dixton Hill was, in any case, almost finished and Father came back with the water cart and horse and the timber yard was slacking off because they could not get timber.

I was then out of work for about a month and I was expected to do odd jobs around the house in general and gardening in part payment for my food because there was no dole money for boys and girls under 18 years of age. Parents were expected to keep their children.

Now, one Friday night when Father came home from the Northwick Brick and Tile Works where he worked as a lorry driver, he said to Mother and me that he had managed to secure me a job at the Brick Works and that I was to report at the office at 7 o'clock on the Monday morning. The hours were 7 a.m. to 5 p.m. Monday to Friday and 7 a.m. to 1 p.m. on Saturdays with no Sunday work. I saw the Yard Foreman and I was instructed as to what my duties consisted of and the rate of pay per hour. I was taken and shown the job which consisted of my having to work with an older man on the brick crushing machine, grinding all the over burnt bricks, half bricks and broken tiles and pipes which was eventually mixed with green clay which was being made into further bricks and tiles.

My rate of pay was 19 shillings a week, 3 shillings better off than the last job at Butlers.

I worked at this job for just over 12 months when the Foreman came to me and asked if I would like another job in another department which had become vacant with about 2 shillings more pay per week. I was given time to think about it and next morning I changed to working 'day work' on the brick press (with 3 more chaps of around my age). The machine pressed green machine-made bricks into imitation handmade bricks. After several weeks of day work, us four chaps were asked if we would consider taking the job piecework at a price we could all agree upon. We, therefore all unanimously agreed to do the job for the price of around 25 shillings per thousand which I must say was very good pay in those days.

The winter of 1929 was hard and after a dry summer, it became snowy and freezing with temperatures in some parts of the country reaching -17 degrees (Ross on Wye).

They came back in the Lorry (my Grandfather drove the Scammell Brick lorry) as far as Snugborough at night. Then it got too bad and *'we had notice to say the Brickyard was going to shut because bricks and clay hole were frozen solid. The clay could not be moved from the clay face and it was no good making bricks with frozen stuff'.*

'All the workers were on the dole, Tile Makers, Brick Makers, setters and everyone and the little kilns were out for a month.'

The Council did employ 3 gangs to dig the Greenway out from Elm Tree to main road and to dig Blockley Hill (The Cross) from Blockley Court to Turnpike and Blockley Street from Elm Tree to Dovedale. Four men from Draycott dug the Draycott road out including Bert Gasside and an old man and Tommy Cross, from Draycott to Cemetery".

"Each side of Blockley Street was piled with snow and way cleared just for traffic. Horse and trolley, everything else had to have chains on. When Dennis Rouse could get out, I helped repair several sets of chains because if they were not pulled tight enough round the tyres they would hit the mudguards and break'.

'It took a bloody long while for the frost to give up. Had to go down to the Station to fetch water with sledges and a bit of board strapped to shoes. Then it started to clear up and we went on for Threshing to fill in time before the brickworks started up again.'

My Father became friends with Jack Franklin the Blacksmith there and they worked together at times. Jack Franklin taught my Father quite a lot about metalwork. He would make moulds for the hand-makers to use. My Father said he was a very good Blacksmith. My Father did not think he was married but he had a very good housekeeper. All his sandwiches were wrapped up.

It came about that Captain Churchill had originally purchased a Steam Engine to run the mill machinery and also bring cars of clay up the gantry from the clay pit. This Engine had come via a Quarry in Wales, from a Steamship and its Engineer had followed his Engine where-ever it went. My Father never told me the name of the Engineer but suffice to say my Father soon learnt everything there was to know about his engine and how it worked and about how the mill machinery worked and how to make brick moulds and do general blacksmithing.

After the big Hoffman Kiln had been built and had been in production for some years. Churchill decided to build what was called 'the little kilns' to produce tiles and odd stuff. These kilns were built, but not without mishap at one point the rooves caved in and had to be rebuilt. These 'little kilns' were never particularly successful but, even though in disrepair, were not removed from the Brickworks until the 1960's.

The Mill machinery was provided by Wootton Brothers of Coalville, Leicestershire and I know for a fact that they were still maintaining this equipment in the late 1960's. (I worked in the office as Secretary to the General Manager, then, Brian Warby and met young Mr. Wootton.)

Father also recalled that Churchill used to come down on the Fast 12 Train from London. (The Fast 12 because it used to get into Moreton-in-Marsh at 12.00 noon, from London, Paddington.). When the train went through Blockley Station, they knew that Churchill's car would be coming through the gate at the Brickworks. Of course, he went straight to the Office to meet, Jack Hull, the Manager and also 'Old Man Brookes' who had worked at a brickworks in the black country and who had been hired for his expertise as Foreman at the brickworks by Captain Churchill.

Captain Churchill decided to replace the Steam Engine with Electric Motors and sold the Steam Engine to a Quarry in Wales and its Engineer 'followed his engine' and went with it.

Captain Churchill had a 100 horse power electric motor installed and because this needed another motor to start it, also had what my Father called a 'trailing 40 horse power motor' installed as well. Knowing my Father's interest in and expertise with engines (my Father was also responsible and reliable) he was asked to take responsibility for all the equipment on the site.

I stayed on that (on the brick press) job for about 8 months until early in 1935 when I was around 23 years of age and I was then asked by the management if I would consider taking over control of all the electrical motors, greasing and oiling all machinery, bearings and setting the brick cutting wires on common brick making machine to the appropriate required sizes also the water pumps in the clay hole and maintenance of air compressors and spades for clay hole use.

The job also required me to be the official time keeper, sounding the compressed air hooter at 7 a.m. start, 9 a.m. break to 9.30 a.m. and 1 p.m. to 2 p.m. lunch and again at 5 p.m. to finish work. For this work I was paid the sum of 35 shillings per 48 hour working week which meant a rise for me again of around 5 shillings per week With the exception of some Saturday afternoons overtime I was able to work another two hours making my weekly hours up to around 50 hours, therefore my pay was up to around £2.00. This suited me fine because at long last I was able to feel more independent and to buy my own clothes of my own choice. The exception I must add was my surgical right boot which I am pleased to say Father and Mother still helped pay somewhat towards that.

It came about that I was in command of that mechanical job until the outbreak of the Second World War in 1939 when everything concerned with the making of bricks, tiles pipes and odd stuff, began to gradually grind to a halt. Men at the brickworks were being called up for service, orders for products declined and coal for burning was not available'. Coal rationing was introduced in 1941 (Miners were being called up for War Service).

I happened to be lucky in one respect that I was kept in work at the brickworks for a while longer. Then as the brickworks finally finished production and ground to a halt by mid-1941, the government took over the brickworks as storage depot for empty ammunition shell cases of all dimensions and sizes. Some of the employees whom were not fit for military service were therefore kept on (I was) and engaged in the unloading storage and cleaning of the ammunition shell cases. This was paid as day work My Father notes; *'July 2 1941. It was day work from this week on and also Ammo Work until Aug 8 1941 when we were sacked from The Brickyard owing to war conditions.'*

I must say the job did not last for long because I was called upon to attend a medical centre board at Gloucester to see if I was capable for enlistment into one of the forces.

I did not pass the fitness medical examination, so was discharged ('sine die') with the grade of B which meant I was capable of doing other war work of some description which would help the war effort. With that medical report, I together with six more of my mates were given our redundancy orders from the Northwick Brick and Tile works and told to report to the local labour exchange at Moreton-in-Marsh'

In a record he kept at the time my Father notes*: Aug 9 1941, I started at the Moreton-in-Marsh Aerodrome for the Electrical Installations Ltd.* He notes: *'First lot of money for Aug., Sept., Oct. and two weeks in November not kept account of but could be put at a steady 4£ per week. But From Nov. 14 1941 have kept account of.* He also notes: *'Went up to Camp from Moreton 5th Jan. First Week P.O.W. (Prisoner of War) Camp Bourton on Hill.*

PART 3

THE FAMILY MOVE TO PITT COTTAGE, BLOCKLEY IN APRIL, 1928

The year that my Father started work at Butler's Timber Yard in 1927, his Sister, Lizzie was married on the 26th February, 1927.

I have written that my Father was very fond of his big Sister, Elizabeth 'Our Lizzie' and he helped her move into, what is now called 'Hop Tree Cottage' on the Springhill Estate with her husband, Charles Henry Taylor. My Father helped her to move some belongings and furniture to the cottage.

'Lizzie' died in March, 1928 and was buried in Blockley Cemetery on the 21st March, 1928, shortly after they had moved to Aston Magna. (My Father always felt that his Sister 'lost the baby and died' because of moving furniture during this move). My Grandparents paid Charles Keyte the Wheelwright and Undertaker for her funeral.

My Father felt this loss profoundly. He did not, however, attend the funeral and could not remember why this was so. I believe, my Father would have been working at Northwick Brickworks by this time and possibly because of his closeness to his Sister his parents may have considered it too much for him to attend.

'Lizzie' outside Hop Tree Cottage just after her marriage in 1927.

My Grandparents paid for the funeral and my Father used to reflect that very few of her belongings were returned to his parents and Charles Taylor remarried, Muriel Honour on 1st August, 1929. 'Lizzie' made her own Wedding Dress, in the 'flapper' style, from silk sent back from Burma by her older Brother, William. At the time of writing in 2023, the dress is with Notty Hornblower at her Costume Museum in Derbyshire. I hope that it will remain there safely and if the contents of the museum are ever sold, it goes on as a remnant of the life of my Father's lovely Sister 'Our Lizzie'.

At the end of April, 1928 the family bought Pitt Cottage, High Street, Blockley, for the sum of £60.00 from Mr. Andrews, who formerly lived at Tredwells, but had moved to 2 Florence Road, Erdington, Birmingham. I have the letter that Mr. Andrews wrote dated 20th April, 1928 acknowledging receipt of the sum of £6.00 as a deposit on the sale of the Cottage.

The cottage had been let to the Gasside family before my Grandfather purchased it. The Cottage was semi-derelict, the back wall of the cottage had fallen out, the fireplace was in poor condition and the Cotswold stone wall around the property was down. The vault toilet outside in a stone shed back-to-back with next door was full to overflowing.

There was already a brick wall built to the side of the back door which cut off access to what is now Middle Cottage where, at that time, Herbert Payne and his wife used to live and this put half of the back wall of Pitt Cottage into the garden of Middle Cottage.

The family were not able to move straight into the cottage immediately. My Grandfather built a garage of corrugated tin in the yard. I think my Grandfather had help building the shed from Fred Mayo who lived across the road in one of the cottages at what is now Rock Bank.

The family lived and cooked in the corrugated tin garage while they were sorting out the cottage and emptying the vault toilet.

Fortuitously there was a huge pile of ashes in the yard, so my Grandfather put a layer of ashes on the 'trolley'. The 'trolley' was pulled by 'Jimmy' the pony who he had purchased and brought back from Birmingham when he was discharged from the hospital in 1920 after WW1.

So, Grandfather began to dig out the vault toilet and pile it on top of the ashes with another layer of ashes on top. My Father related that my grandfather's stomach was 'not strong' so to cope, he got 'his old pipe going'. The further down they dug the darker and smellier it became. My Grandfather could not continue with digging it out so my father finished the job. He said they took several loads up on to the Warren with 'Jimmy and the Trolley' and spread it up there.

The place where the old vault toilet had been was filled in with earth and stone from the Cotswold stone wall that had surrounded the side and back of the cottage. Uncle Joe (Grandfather's brother Joseph Hicks) came and helped Grandfather build a new brick wash-house and toilet from common bricks my grandfather purchased from Northwick Brick and Tile Works where he worked as a Lorry Driver.

A flush toilet was installed, albeit in those days, a bucket of water was carried out to flush it. A new wall to replace the Cotswold Stone wall between what was the old hurdle maker's yard and the wall at the side of Brook Lane was built about 3 feet high from 'brick seconds' from the Northwick Brick and Tile Works.

(It is just within my memory that there was a large Walnut Tree where Laggan Cottage Garage now stands and that a Gypsy Caravan belonging to Mr. Paintin who lived in Fulbrook Cottage stood under it.)

The Wash-house and Tin Garage were also joined by a Greenhouse situated outside the backdoor which was linked to the Wash-house by another tinned roofed shed which held wood and logs for the fire and also the swill bin for the pig swill.

(When I was small, we used to cut up the Daily Express (then a Broadsheet) for toilet paper and put a hole in the corner of the paper for the piece of string to go through. Granny kept the soft wrapping paper from oranges and any tissue that came into the house for herself).

My Father moved back to Pitt Cottage in 1971 with his wife, Dora, to look after his mother who died in March, 1978. She is buried with her daughter, Elizabeth, in Blockley Cemetery.

I have lived at Pitt Cottage since I returned home in 1984.

BETWEEN THE WARS

Although my Father did leave extensive notes about his working life during the period between the Wars (World War 1 and World War 2). He did not write extensively about his social life but from conversations I had with him, when he was not helping out his Mother and Father with the pigs and chickens on the land they rented on the Warren and at Pinners Quarry, he occasionally forayed out to the local public houses and to the 'pictures' in Moreton-in-Marsh, with some of his mates from the Brickworks. He was, however, always very careful with his money and spent very little for his own personal entertainment.

My Grandfather and Grandmother who had saved to purchase Pitt Cottage outright in 1928, also owned a car from a very early date.

Initially, my Grandfather had purchased a 'Delm' Motorbike on which my Grandmother and Grandfather used to travel to London to see his brother (Uncle Joe). Then he bought a BSA Motorbike straight from the factory in Birmingham. He had to have the passenger seat of this modified by Jack Franklin the Blacksmith at the Brickworks and a handle fitted for my Grandmother to hold because she did not like holding him round his waist. After my Grandfather sold the motor bike he bought a 3 wheeled Morgan. (At the time my Grandfather had given up the ground rented from Northwick on the Warren and had moved to Pinner's Quarry). The Morgan had one wheel at the rear and two at the front. So that they could get along Donkey Lane to Pinner's Quarry easily, my Grandfather and Father dug a channel in the grass in the centre of the lane. They were admonished for this by the Farm Manager and told to put it back. (It did not go back).

After the Morgan my Grandfather bought an Austin 7 Saloon. In the early 1930's my Father and Grandfather travelled to see Aston Villa play at their home ground of Villa Park, in this vehicle, and my Father recalls that they 'conked' for petrol on the way back, possibly because someone had syphoned some out of the tank. However, Grandfather was familiar with the area (from driving the brick lorry) and they soon got the car filled up again and back on their way home).

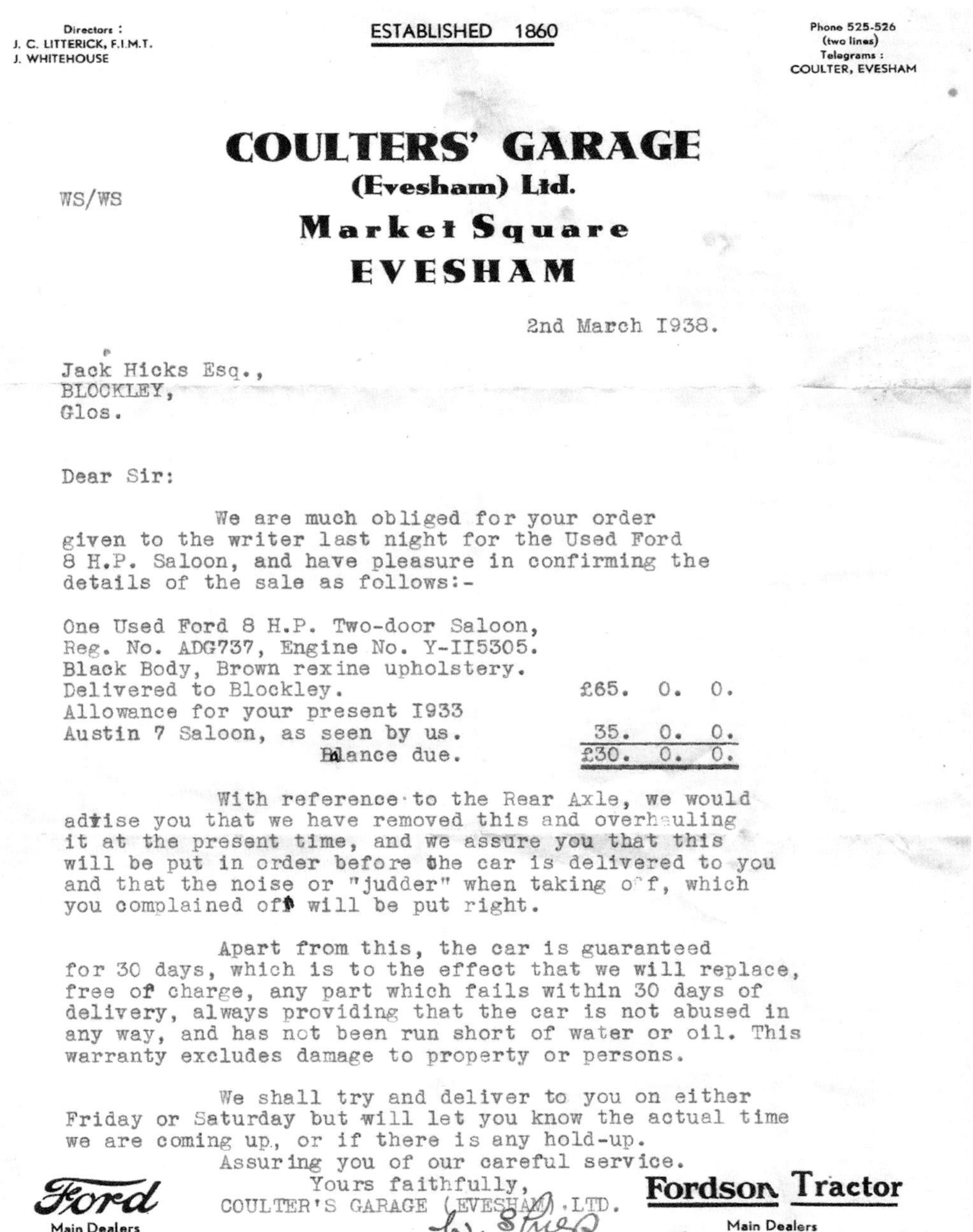

Directors:
J. C. LITTERICK, F.I.M.T.
J. WHITEHOUSE

ESTABLISHED 1860

Phone 525-526
(two lines)
Telegrams:
COULTER, EVESHAM

COULTERS' GARAGE
(Evesham) Ltd.
Market Square
EVESHAM

WS/WS

2nd March I938.

Jack Hicks Esq.,
BLOCKLEY,
Glos.

Dear Sir:

We are much obliged for your order given to the writer last night for the Used Ford 8 H.P. Saloon, and have pleasure in confirming the details of the sale as follows:-

One Used Ford 8 H.P. Two-door Saloon,
Reg. No. ADG737, Engine No. Y-II5305.
Black Body, Brown rexine upholstery.

Delivered to Blockley.	£65. 0. 0.
Allowance for your present I933 Austin 7 Saloon, as seen by us.	35. 0. 0.
Balance due.	£30. 0. 0.

With reference to the Rear Axle, we would advise you that we have removed this and overhauling it at the present time, and we assure you that this will be put in order before the car is delivered to you and that the noise or "judder" when taking off, which you complained of, will be put right.

Apart from this, the car is guaranteed for 30 days, which is to the effect that we will replace, free of charge, any part which fails within 30 days of delivery, always providing that the car is not abused in any way, and has not been run short of water or oil. This warranty excludes damage to property or persons.

We shall try and deliver to you on either Friday or Saturday but will let you know the actual time we are coming up, or if there is any hold-up.
Assuring you of our careful service.

Yours faithfully,
COULTER'S GARAGE (EVESHAM) LTD.
W. Spiers

Ford
Main Dealers

Fordson Tractor
Main Dealers

Letter from Coulter's Garage for purchase of Ford 8 H.P Motor Car

On the 2nd March, 1938 my Grandfather traded in this Austin 7 Saloon for £35.00 and bought a used Ford 8 horsepower, two door saloon, Registration No. ADG 737 Engine No. Y11305, Black Body, Brown Rexine Upholstery, from Coulters Garage, Market Square, Evesham. The car cost £60.00 but with the trade in he only paid £30.00. (Still a considerable sum of money in those days).

Also in 1938 My Grandfather was given Notice to leave the ground at Pinner's Quarry that they had rented for a number of years and used as a garden and kept Pigs and chicken's on. A copy of the Notice given on Lady Day 1938 to quit Pinner's Quarry on 25th March, 1939. A house was built on the site of 'in my Father's words' the best bit of the garden ground up there.

51A, LINCOLN'S INN FIELDS,

LONDON, W.C.2.

As Agents for and on behalf of

CAPTAIN E. G. S-CHURCHILL, M.C.

WE HEREBY GIVE YOU NOTICE to quit and yield up, on the twenty-fifth day of March, 1939, possession of the Messuage, with its appurtenances, lands, tenements, and hereditaments, which you now hold of Captain Churchill, situate and being Ord. No. 174 (Pinners Quarry) in the Parish of Blockley in the County of Gloucestershire

Dated this First day of September 1938.

To Mr. Jack Hicks.

PART 4

WARTIME 1940 TO 1945

My Father notes: *It came about that I was drafted into a new employment which was totally very different altogether to what I had been accustomed to.*

There were about 8 men that my Father worked with at the brickworks that had to finish. The Head Foreman (Jack Hull) came round on the Monday when we got there. He said *'you young chaps (Tiddley White, Parker and Percy Eastbury, me and old Fletch had got to finish on Monday morning and you must report to the dole office on Friday, but you will have to take your cards with you when you go to Moreton Labour Exchange in the afternoon.*

When we got to the Labour Exchange, old 'Randy' Haines said to us when we went in 'they need some men up at Moreton Aerodrome' and he gave us a gate pass, a green card, each and on a Saturday morning in the month of August 1941 *we all biked up there to report to the Foreman of the Electrical Installations Limited which happened to be contracted on the newly built RAF Station at Moreton-in-Marsh.*

('Tiddley' White lived in the then tramway crossing house on the main Fosse Way near Shipston on Stour and Parker lived at Todenham. Percy Eastbury lived in Blockley and 'Fletch' lived in Paxford.)

My Father's 'old pal' Fletch.

The Foreman's first words to all of us were 'when can you make a start'. We replied that we could start straight away if he could provide us with some sort of a mid-day meal, and he said he thought he could arrange that with the NAAFI for 12.30 p.m. which he did.

We thought we would become full blown Electricians in a few minutes (so to speak) but there was a big shock awaiting all of us, especially me, because together with my other colleagues we were handed a shovel each and conducted to a trench in the ground and told to start and back-cover electric cables which had been placed in the trench.

This was my first whole Saturday working day for a good many years and the time seemed to drag tremendously until around 4.30 p.m. when the Site Foreman returned and said we could all knock off until the Monday morning at 8 a.m.

When I finally arrived home that same Saturday at around 5.15 p.m. Mother seemed as though she had been worrying to some extent and she wanted to know straight away how things had progressed for me. I answered her question by saying 'I had managed to secure further employment with an Electrical Installation Firm on Moreton-in-Marsh Airfield'.

I together with one of my mates who lived in the village reported for work again the following Monday morning at 8 a.m. (which seemed strange because I had been starting work at 7 a.m. at the Brick Yard.). We were told by the site foreman to resume working where we had left off on the previous Saturday afternoon.

This work seemed very funny to me and my mates because we had all been accustomed to working indoors, therefore being drafted to working outdoors, I can tell you took some getting acclimatised towards.

In the first instance I used to have my shirt sleeves cut off short for inside work and when it came about we had to work outdoors my arms and face started to peel due to the sunshine burning them. I had to ask Mother if she would be kind enough to sew the cut off part of my shirt sleeves back on again. I am pleased to say she did so to help save the agony the sun was doing to my skin. After about a month I was getting to enjoy working out of doors after about 14 years working inside buildings, therefore as winter started to creep along it did not seem to be so noticeable.

Together with my mates, I continued laying cables and back-covering them, at Moreton Airfield until our firm had nearly completed the work. Now, on reporting for work again one Monday morning in January 1942, the Site Foreman, together with one of our District Electrical Engineers approached us and asked the four of us if we would like to make a start on a new site at Bourton on the Hill German Prisoner of War site working on electrical overhead mains installations but first of all he said, 'think it over and let me know by Wednesday night of the same week'. After they were gone we resumed our old workings and discussed all the details concerning the job and our form of travel and the distance involved. Well, at last our decision was made with the result that when the District Engineer came again to me and the others on the Wednesday we put our case to him stating the idea would be okay for my Blockley mates and me but the other two would have to cycle nearly ten miles each way, morning and night. After putting our point of view to him it was finally decided for me and my local mate to transfer to the new site at Bourton on the Hill P.O.W. camp and that the full 4 man compliment could be made up by engaging two more men which lived as close to the site as we did. Therefore, with that all decided upon, my two other old workmates had to stay behind on odd jobbing bits of cable runs at Moreton-in-Marsh, RAF Station.

So, from the January of 1942 until the end of December 1942, I, together with my other mates were engaged on the overhead electrical wiring system at the Prisoner of War site at Bourton on the Hill. The work was very hard; digging holes 5 ft. deep and helping to erect the wooden poles and run the electric bare copper wire off the drums and proceed with it up through the insulators on the erected poles. For this kind of work we all were entitled to the London Electrical workmen's rate of pay, not the local rate, because, being as our electrical firm was a London firm we were entitled to that rate of pay.

Everything had been going along very smoothly for several months and also the work was running up to schedule, until one day the District Engineer came to us all again and mentioned that some 36 concrete poles were due on the site to help finish the job off 'pole wise' as wood poles were getting extremely hard to buy due to the war time economy. After the Engineer had gone, we began to discuss the matter of this concrete pole erecting episode between ourselves and other site workers. Eventually we all came to same conclusion that the job should be talked over between the management and ourselves to the extent that, I, together with all my mates should get the concrete pole erecting job entered under the Constructional Engineering side of the business because anything solid like the concrete poles, iron work or any other solid matter came under a different heading as regards payment of wages. So, it was decided between the four of us to ask our site foreman if we could have an interview with the District Engineer when he was due on the site again (which was in about 3 days time). so that we could put our point of view to him as regards extra payment for undertaking the task of erecting the concrete poles.

Well, on the day when the District Engineer came the site foreman brought the engineer to see us. We, sedately at first, put our point of view and suggestions to him concerning the erection of the concrete poles, BUT I am afraid the conversation soon led into a slanging match with some very unpleasant remarks being made towards us four and management which resulted into nothing being finalised by either party. On this occasion we just parted with leaving everything in abeyance until a further meeting could be called. In the meantime, the concrete poles were not being erected, and only the ordinary routine work was being done with the wooden poles and overhead runs.

Whilst the concrete pole erection was being kept in abeyance by us, in the hope that we would get our own way and also more money in the finish, I, together with my other mates were quietly gathering further information from the other workmen and other firms site foremen and also we sent away to Her Majesty's Stationery Office in London for a book of rules and regulations concerning nearly everything of the nature which we required for our case. Now, it was back to square one again for us on receiving all that further information. So, therefore, on presenting ourselves for work again one Monday morning all the four of us awaited the arrival of the Site Foreman so that we could present our further case to him again concerning the concrete poles. At last, he came and found us, not on our jobs at work but sitting in the hut. "Hello", he says, also using swear words as well, and what do you think you lot are up to, you should be out doing your work. Now when he had calmed down some-what we could start to approach him in the proper manner. He was asked by one of us , if he would please make another appointment for us to see the District Engineer again as we had another proposition to put to him when he comes up to the site on Wednesday again.

After talking at length *and threatening which became as high as nearly punching the foreman on the nose, he reluctantly said he would phone up and see if another appointment could be made with the District Engineer, me and the other chaps. The Site Foreman said to us if we would return to our jobs straight away he would phone up and let us know the result by lunch time 'therefore' on that promise we did venture out of the hut and resumed our work. He kept his promise and phoned up with the result that the District Engineer would see us . Well, I must say everything went off very smoothly for the next two days. Therefore, when the Engineer did come of the Wednesday, I, together with the other three was summoned to see him in the hut in the presence of the Site Foreman. On arriving at the hut we could see that his previous attitude had not changed much. From his chair he said 'sit down and what is it you wish to see me about'. I thought 'look out'. He said, 'If I think what it is then the answer is No, which I must say came as a bit of a shock to me and my mates until we recovered somewhat, whilst he was still relating the pay scales for this and the pay rules for that. We waited until he had his say and was about to rise from his chair when I thought we would fire our bomb shell at him and await the immediate results from him. So out comes our book of knowledge and also asking his permission if we could read Chapter so and so, paragraph so and so to him to which he consented. The chapter and paragraph was read to him concerning the erection of iron, concrete and wooden poles or supports' As it was beginning to be read to him I could see his face changing colour with practically every word. When the reading was finished he sat quiet for several minutes then said, 'before anything else, where did you lot get that book of information from as you have no rights with it'. By that time his face was nearly scarlet red 'as they are only supposed to be only available for our managerial side'. I and my mates therefore once again awaited for him also by now the Site Foreman whom had started to interfere to calm down a bit so that all of us together could start and talk some common-sense concerning the extra money for constructional erecting of the said items.*

At last, after a little further conversation from him, he condescended to meet our requirements for the extra money because it was, as he said 'being as we four were armed with the book of further information it would be useless for him to deny us the payment for job which amounted to an extra 2d per hour, which meant an extra 20 old pence in our 10 hour days work. Now, when he agreed to pay us the extra money, he stipulated that it would only be for the duration of the concrete pole erection period. To this stipulation we readily agreed. Therefore, with this episode finally cleared up and our case won we went back out and resumed our left off jobs until such times it was convenient for us to start to erect the concrete poles.

It came about just after the Easter holiday of April, 1942. I together with my mates received instruction both from the District Engineer and the Site Foreman that we were to get everything prepared which we thought was needed for the erection of the concrete poles to make a start on them. So, a list was started by us in respect of the requirements, such as ropes to act as guided ropes, iron pegs which was to drive into the ground to help steady the poles when being erected and other numerous gadgets, such as iron bars for leverage and sledge hammers and last but not least some very strong men.

Well, for me, together with my mates and site foreman at last came the day of reckoning . We were ready for the first concrete pole erection. All the holes had been excavated out down to the depth of 5 ft. 6 inches. This depth was needed because each pole weighed one ton 5 cwts and were 30 feet long overall, the height of the pole out of the ground had to clear 24 ft 6 inches for road clearance and also ground clearance after the 3 phase and one neutral line were added it had to have a clearance of 21 ft, so one can tell what had to be contended with as well. Well now, this is where the fun started. I together with my mates were all given different tasks to do in the preparation for the first erection. I was given the task of securing four ropes at different angles to the pole, to act as guides and steadying anchors. My local mate was given a sledge hammer and told to drive four iron pegs into the ground (the pegs were four feet long at different angles to act as the anchors on erection and after erection, the other three men were preparing the hole, plank of wood to help slide the pole down into the hole and also a very strong short ladder we had managed to cadge for one chap to help 'scotch up' behind when a rest was needed by the lifters (that happened to be my position when erection was taking place) of the concrete one ton five hundred weight poles.

Now me and my mates plus the foreman are all set for the lift off. Firstly, everything was going according to plan until we had to get the concrete pole up practically halfway. It was then that some of the problems started for me because in the first place as I had been scotching up behind, I happened to notice that none of the guide ropes were even taking some of the weight and strain and it happened to be four strong sturdy chaps which had been lifting. They, was, by now, not being able to lift any more because of the height and the angle of the pole. Therefore. that left me with the whole weight of the pole upon the little ladder I was scotching up with and another thing was, which made it more dangerous for us, was the pole had not started to bottom into the hole properly as it had slipped off the plank in to the side of the bank of the hole which I must say was making things more difficult for us to erect. Now, I shouted to my mates to get out of the way because of the danger (to which they did at once) that the ladder may break under the strain. Then. after a minute or two. we found that the ladder was taking the strain very well, hereafter it was decided that more strength was needed to help lift the pole upright out of that precarious position. So, whilst we had blowings and a bit of tobacco – off went our foreman in search of another contractors site foreman to ask if he would condescend to let us have three or four of his men to give us a hand with the final lift. In the meantime whilst he was away my mates and I put some more wood planks which were available under the end of the concrete pole as well as the ladder to help take the strain and weight off the small ladder.

Well. after some considerable time of waiting. back comes our foreman together with what all of us estimated was four of the strongest Irishmen on the whole site. Therefore. after some discussion with us and the foreman as to our needs, they just said 'sure and begorra its nothing but a matchstick, one of them said 'Right Ho' me hearties, up and under it' they put their shoulders to it and in no time at all the concrete pole was stood upright in the hole awaiting to be back filled.

Now all this strength and ability rocked our foreman to the roots of his boots with the exclamation of 'you four are the ones we would like for this erection job'. 'Ho now, me-matey' said their spokesman in a flash to our foreman.' We'll tell you what us four will do. How many poles have you to erect,' 35 now, was the foreman's reply . Therefore, after a bit of consultation between themselves, their spokesman said ' every time you needs a pole erecting let us know and we will come and help erect it with you for say around £1.00 per pole which meant five shillings per person. Now that of course took our foreman by surprise with the result that he said he would let them know definite in another day or two. They said 'OK', after being given a cigarette each, so away they went. After they had gone the foreman had a little talk with us four, and asked us our opinion, if we would be in agreement with the Irishman's suggestion. Our answer to this question was 'we thought it would be a very good idea if things could be arranged for the four Irishmen to have the money as their extra help would be very much appreciated and also a time saving factor, being as they were willing to come and help. So, with that thought in mind, the foreman went again to the four Irishmen's site foreman to talk over the agreement which the four Irishmen had suggested. The two foremen must have come to some agreement between themselves as regards payment for the four extra hands, because after that day, every time there was another pole ready for erection which needed the other extra hands, we had only to let the four men's site foremen know first thing in the morning about what time we would be ready for a lift and the extra hands were there.

Now, before we started backfilling the first concrete post hole, the foreman said he believed the instructions on the plan concerning the backfilling of the concrete pole holes stated that the first two feet six inches of the pole hole were to be of concrete and not stone and dirt like the wooden pole holes, therefore whilst me, together with my other mates were preparing another pole ready for erection he would just go back to our hut and consult the plan which governed the job.

After some considerable time he came back to us and said 'that he was quite right about the depth of concrete into the hole first and then the stones and dirt, so with that information which he passed on to us, we were able to complete the first concrete pole erection,

Now, with that pole erected and also with all that extra information gathered, we, that is my mates and myself were able to move onto the next pole for erection. Well, I must say with that information gathered we very soon started to get into difficulties with the second pole, everything was put in working order so we thought, the four extra lifters had been fetched and the lifting started, when all of a sudden the concrete pole gave a sudden lurch to one side, which caused all the lifters to fall over the opposite side to which the pole fell back to the ground. It's a good job the pole did not fall the same side as all of us, because it was then that I hated what might have happened to myself and my mates. After myself and mates had gathered themselves together it was found that the two back guide ropes had dislodged themselves from their mooring stakes. After those had been moored safely again and I and my mates together with the four other men started another lift it was found that the concrete pole had been cracked straight through the middle when it fell down onto the hard ground. That of course caused another upstart because by being cracked it was of no further use and also there happened to be no spare replacements. So, to amend matters as best as was possible the foreman went and contacted our head office in Vincent Square London on the phone to ask their advice as regards making the pole useable again. When he came back to us with the information he had received it was to say, strap the pole on either side with half inch thick by four inch wide steel flat bars and use four half inch thick by twelves inches long steel nuts and bolts. In other words strap the pole so that the crack was in the middle of the straps and also paint straps and bolts with weather resistant paints. By this time, it was nearly going home time for that day, therefore we just left everything where it was and went home.

Now on the following morning my mates and myself were told to go and prepare another pole for erection. The Foreman went down to the Moreton-in-Marsh Blacksmiths for the nuts, bolts and strap iron and also the loan of a half inch masonry drill for the drilling through the concrete pole to assesmble the strap irons. By the time we had finished our preparations on the next pole it was nearly break time (around ten o clock) for a cup of tea and a sandwich or two. Therefore, as we made our way back towards our hut we noticed that the foreman was back and was busy together with the blacksmith whom had accompanied the foreman back up to undertake the job of repairing the cracked pole.

During breaktime we were visited in the hut by the foreman to say in about one hour from now the cracked pole will be ready for erection again and would one of us go and notify the other four helping lifters to be ready in the meantime. My mates and I were to prepare stakes ropes and so forth at the cracked pole ready for lift off again.

Well now, when everything was ready again everybody was given their positions (even the old Blacksmith) for the lift off. Therefore, on the word of command from the Foreman everyone took the strain and lifted the pole just as though it was a little bird. Therefore, in no time at all the pole was upright. The Blacksmith was taken back to Moreton-in-Marsh and the first two foot six inches of wet concrete to be inserted into the hole. With that the pole was completed and backfilled. I together with my mates moved on to the next and then the next and so forth until the 36 concrete poles had been erected without, I am very pleased to say any further mishap like letting any more fall.

Now, after that strenuous work had been accomplished I with my mates next job was to start the running out of the bare copper cables off the drums and erect them upon the poles, ready for the linesmen to make secure, through the porcelain insulators with 14 gauge copper binding wire.

This being all done in the matter of a few months, our next task was to take the VIR covered insulated wire runs from the pole insulators to the Nissen huts pole and make them off. That is where our contract finished at every hut pole. Beyond that point it became the indoor electrician's job to make the rest good and in working order.

Now it was nearly the end of December, 1942 and we were nearing completion of the German Prisoner of War Camp at Bourton on the Hill, with the exception of one or two huts because they had not been completely built and also with the exception of some cleaning up, such as cable drums, ladders, planks and so forth.

Well, now, two days before Christmas of that year, just after my mates and I had been paid by the outside Foreman (with the money which came from London head office each week) he said that our District Engineer was making a call and would like all of us to be in the hut, or thereabouts around 3 p.m. because he had something to offer which might be in our favour.

Now my mates and I discussed this information at some length because we thought it may consist of a bonus or some sort in recognition of the hard work we had done in erecting the concrete poles or some form of Christmas Bonus. But that was not so, because by the time it was three o'clock we had all assembled in our hut awaiting the arrival of the District Engineer, it was to learn when he did finally arrive and present his speech, that it was not a Christmas Bonus or any other form of payment in recognition of services rendered but only to tell me and my mates that he had other electrical work employment on another site for us now that Bourton the Hill P.O.W site was very near completion. Now after being stunned to the depths of our boots, my mates and I asked what the other job consisted of and where was it situated, locally or where have you.

Whilst I together with my mates were considering these things over a little, the District Engineer and also the site foreman were talking amongst themselves about something we could not hear. Therefore, by the time they had finished talking and us likewise, the Engineer turned to me and my mates and said that he had got two jobs in the pipe line which needed an extra couple of three extra hands each, therefore would us four be willing to split up into two gangs and therefore two to go to one place and work whilst the other two of you goes to the other place to help out. But he also added this ultimatum with his speech and this was 'Should you not decide to split up into two gangs and go to the two different places he would only have to phone up the labour exchange concerning if we were to refuse and it would therefore come about that we could be conscripted because it was wartime and one had to work where labour was needed most if none existed in ones living area'. Now, as we thought together that did not leave my mates and I much room to manoeuvre as regards refusing because just around that war time period there was very little work around in the Blockley area to be had. So, after some more severe talk between the engineer and foreman my mates and I asked where the other jobs were going and whom of us four had to split up.

Well now, the cheeky 'b' of an engineer said, we are just beginning to talk sense at last. He said (us, alluding to my Blockley mate and myself, could go down to Pershore Aerodrome on underground cabling jointing and assisting two underground jointers. The other two of my mates could either go back to the Moreton-in-Marsh Aerodrome site for two weeks or go straight on to a new site at Deddington near to Banbury. He added this little bit of unnecessary news as well. 'You all will be expected to live away from home from Monday morning until Friday night or perhaps Saturday mid-day whichever working time applies on site at the time'.

Just before he departed from our midst, he gave us this ultimatum, we was to let him know of our discussion by the last two days of December 1942 before we finally pulled out of the POW camp at Bourton on the Hill, so that he could make all the arrangements as regards the accommodation such as meals, sleeping and our welfare in general.

When everything was back to normal again and being as it was very near the Christmas Festive Season, we all, (that is my mates and I) just sat down and therefore just quietly talked things over for the next one and a half days to just try to work out the situation as far as we could see it, such as where we would be gaining and losing and also if we were all of one mind as regarding having to live away from home.

Well, I must say that I together with my mates and also I must say with some assistance from our Site Foreman whom we brought into the conversation, we thought very deeply into the matter and therefore we finally agreed between ourselves we would all give it a trial period of about a month and then if not satisfied with the conditions we would ask for a transfer to another suitable worksite position in the company or into another employment somewhere else.

Well now, the time finally arrived for us when we had to notify the District Engineer of our discussions that we my mate and I would take the Pershore job on a months trial, therefore also both of us would live away from home during the week and returning home every Friday night or Saturday mornings. I must say now, those terms were accepted. So on January 4th 1943, I, together with my Blockley mate were picked up from home in the motor car of our old site foreman and conveyed to Pershore Aerodrome and introduced to our new site foreman who conveyed us to our living and sleeping quarters. He also took us to the cookhouse and introduced us to the cook and waitresses which of course were oldish people because nearly all the young and able bodied people had been conscripted into the services of some kind. From there we were told that 'your lot you must make the most of it'.

By now it was dinner time, 12.30 p.m., therefore the foreman said he would treat us to our first dinner on site, if we would oblige him with our company. We accepted his invitation thankfully that we would be able to get any good insight into how my mate and I would have to proceed hereafter. Well after lunch we were escorted on a conducted tour of the whole works site by our site foreman and also introduced to the two underground cable jointers, my mate and I were to work with in the future. After that conducted tour was over, the time was nearing the hour of 4 p.m. with the result that us two was invited into the site forman's office so that we would be favoured for the signing of all the necessary forms and so forth the, as was permissible for everyone entering a new site for employment of any descriptions. It did not matter if it was for the same employer or not because the procedure was the same for the site authorities so that they knew how many people were actively working on the site enbloc.

With that all finished and behind us we were asked to partake of a cup of tea with the site foreman and his female office staff which numbered four. There were two old and two younger ladies who gave all visitors a good impression of the firm they represented because all the time my mate and I were in their presence together with the site foreman, no work was undertaken.

With everything straight and above board, us two were dismissed by our site foreman from his office and told by him the rest of the day was ours to do as we pleased but we were to report at his office by 8 a.m. on the following morning, where together with my mate, we would be assigned to an underground jointer.

Now, this was sort of the beginning of another era for me, because for the first instance I was not prepared to live away from home again as I had some years previous with another firm of timber tree sawyers. Secondly the living conditions were appalling at some of the sites or camps which were being built.

Well, on the Monday night my mate and I made our beds up for the night ready. The time was around 6.30 p.m. Therefore, to help us through the rest of the evening we made talking friends with two more chaps which were in the same predicament as ourselves. We therefore decided to seek out the nearest public house and go for a drink some refreshments and also a game or two of cards, darts or what have you. Now it came about that the other two chaps knew of a pub within walking distance to the site where we were. Therefore, after some more conversation between us we finally made our way over there. Which

I must say was some considerable distance of walking which was around 1 and a half miles we eventually reached our destination with the result that the first pint was only bitten in half once, the second and third drinks went down somewhat of a slower pace until the landlord finally called time, which was 10 p.m in those days, then we had to finally walk back to the site and to bed. I would like to say here and now that not much sleep was forthcoming for me that night for several reasons. First it was not realised by me or my mate during that first day on the site that there would be another 28 men sharing the same sleeping accommodation hut with my mate and myself. Secondly because the beds were hard and lumpy also no sheets were allocated to us. Therefore, that meant us having to sleep between the blankets which numbered four no more which were not very clean to our estimation. On waking somewhere in the region of around 6 a.m. on that following morning, I discovered whilst I was still in bed that it was possible to see the grass and some of the other huts though the big gaps or cracks which were in the sides of the huts, no wonder it was most uncomfortable, and draughty during the night.

Well now being as it was Tuesday and the start of my second day at the site, I thought here goes, so out of bed I gets the time being around 6.15 a.m. (gives my mate a push as he was fast asleep) gets dressed grabs the towel and soap and outside to find my way to the ablutions for a wash and brush up with my mate following close behind.

After all these preliminaries finished back to the hut I went, rolled my bed and bedding up and then grabbed my belongings such as coats and mackintosh, and so forth and away down to the canteen for breakfast.

First choice was fried eggs and bacon, fried bread, together with fried tomatoes or baked beans. Second choice was of porridge, cereals or just bread and butter and marmalade and with as many cups of tea one desired. After these things which had been on display for our convenience so that please ourselves which we would like to partake of had been dispensed with the time was now 7.30 a.m. and time for me and my mate to find the way over the site to our office and report for work to our site foreman.

Now before leaving the canteen the supervisor came over to our table because she knew both my mate and I were two new comers to the site and gave each of us a packet of sandwiches for our midmorning break which was about 10 a.m. . The kind lady also told us two that the cooked midday meal had to be taken in two sessions, the first being at 12.30 p.m. to 1.00 p.m., the second session would begin at 1.15 p.m. until 1.45 p.m. Now the kind lady said we had been included in the first session at 12.30 p.m. for reasons which suited the Electrical Installations best. Therefore, in future she said our table Number would be so and so over in one corner of the very big dining room but today being as it is your first time of dining here I would like you both to honour me with your presence in my office and hoping we would oblige. Well now we thanked her very much and said we would oblige and gathered our packets of sandwiches up and away to our employment.

Well, we reported to the site foreman and were allocated our tradesman underground jointer each. Now as luck would have it, both the underground jointers happened to be working on the same length of cable, therefore after my mate's jointer did their work, with their kit of tools, blow lamps, solder (the white solder jointing) we then jumped up into the motorised truck and away out onto the job on another part of the site where we worked very well together which made it very much pleasanter all around.

Now, this is where I am sorry to say our short-lived friendship came unstuck very soon, because when 10 a.m. came my mate and I thought it perhaps would be breaktime, so that we could have our packed sandwiches. Well 10 a.m. came and went with no sign of my mate making any effort to stop for his break, so at around 10.30 a.m. I found that my tummy was getting hungry . I happened to mention the fact to my jointer mate that it was 10.30 am and time for our usual breaktime to have our prepared sandwiches. Now, I shall never know what he was just thinking at that time, but all of a sudden he looked up at me flabbergasted and said twice 'sandwiches' sandwiches, we don't reckon to break off on this job on site for sandwiches at this time of the morning mate, it is not just done and that's it.

If either you or your mate stop, I will report both of you to my Site Foreman. Now, with that sort of speech which I had just received from him made me start thinking, so I thought, just to hear him right and to make him repeat himself again I said' what did I hear you say that you would report us in for having a sandwich'. Yes, I would, he said and that's that. So. with that threat, being put in my way and also being as I did not like being threatened with those sort of sayings. I immediately put down the things I was holding and went further along the trench to where my mate and his jointer mate were working. On seeing me approaching he wondered what was going on, therefore when I got up to him, I ups and tells them both just what my jointer mate had told me as regards us two or three if we partook of sandwiches at this time of the morning. After both of them had listened to my story concerning the sandwiches the jointer looks up and said to both my mate and myself, 'don't take any notice of him, he has always been like that with all the other chaps whom has been his mates to him'. 'I therefore advise you, just go back up and sit down on something and start eating your sandwiches (as me and mate here are just about to partake of ours) but make sure you watches out for his actions'.

So, with that information gathered I went back up to where my jointer mate was only to find him stood up with his face scowling somewhat and also he started to say 'just where the bloody hell have you been as I have been waiting for some of your assistance with this cable'. I thought by his conversation being as you is in that frame of mind I just will not take any notice of you but therefore just sit down and started eating my sandwiches. Now that done it. All of a sudden I saw his face change colour and out of the trench he jumps. My mate grabs hold of the jointer (my mate was big built) and held him up straight and gave him such a doughboy and knocked him back into the trench with these words to follow 'don't you ever do things like that again or else'. After that episode my mate goes back to his mate leaving me to deal with the spoils he had left in the trench and also the abusive language which was being put forward by him in both of our favours, but I must say it actually quietened him down somewhat as us two mates were told some while after this episode that this jointer had been a somewhat of a trouble maker with different chaps before but after his coming into contact with my mate he began to have different thoughts, also became more pleasant to work with. Now after those first two hectic days on a new site my mate and I were looking forward to more quieter times ahead in the further days to come.

Well now, I would like to say that things did improve tremendously as I am about to describe. My jointer mate after some sulkiness which lasted nearly two days, then suddenly one dinner came over to the meal table where my mate and I sat having our cooked meal (my mate thought he had come for another belting), he sat down and quietly began to talk to us in quite a nice frame of mind of speech.

He began by saying 'had us two been introduced to all the facilities available for us and everybody on the site . We said 'No, 'We had now got with this sudden change in this topic of conversation from him come to us two and it came as quite a surprise, therefore, we thought we had better be on our intuitive guards. Therefore, we just looked on with caution until we could see that he had become more gentle in his manner towards us. Well now after listening to the chap for some considerable time with his rattling on about this and that my mate and I just kindly said to him, 'perhaps in another day or two we would like for him to act as our chaperon for an evening or two to different parts of the site for a picture show or a quiet social evening with some of the other chaps whom were attached to the Electrical Installations.

With that conversation finished my mate and I went back to our sleeping quarters to find out if there were any letters or parcels arrived from home and also to replenish ourselves with some more cigarettes from our locked-up suitcases (It was not safe to leave anything unlocked in those days), and then back outside and quietly proceed back to the work area and our jointer mates.

Now I must say, here and now, that after our big up and downer with the jointer mate it turned out that in the remainder of our working time together he practically came out tops together with my old working mate. Well now the weeks kept coming and going for us two mates, home for the weekend from Pershore Aerodrome, back again on Monday mornings for months and months, in fact it seemed that the job would never end until around August, 1942 when one Thursday afternoon the same District Engineer and Site Foreman came to see all concerned on the site when he enlightened arrangements for my mate and I to go and see him in the offices (my mate thought it was to receive our dismissal notices).

On arriving into the offices we both were told to sit down and make ourselves comfortable because the conversation could be of some length, so both of us obliged and sat down.

Well, 'how do both of you' asked the District Engineer, our reply was 'very well thank you'. Well now the Engineer stated 'I suppose you both knows that your kind of work as underground jointers mates on this site is gradually coming to a close. We said 'yes, we did', he continued,' so therefore, I am going to put two propositions to you both with a thought in my mind that you will think on it for a day or two and let me know the answer though your site foreman here, if you are willing to accept'.

'The first proposition is this. I need two underground cable jointers mates up at Moreton-in-Marsh aerodrome to assist two underground jointers for about 6 to 8 weeks, alternatively, failing to take this job there is the second proposition. You two chaps together with another four whom are now at Moreton completely could go on to a new site at Stanford in the Vale near to Wantage in Berkshire assisting with cable laying and cable jointing. In fact, it is work like the two of you have already been doing. 'Well now', he said at last. 'is there any questions'.

'Ho yes', I said 'plenty'. 'Firstly, what are the travelling facilities concerning each job? What do they consist of?'. 'Well, his reply was to that question, 'firstly I will take the Moreton-in-Marsh site, should you take that. I am afraid you both would have to make your own way to that either by cycle or if either of you are the owner of a car you could use that of course'. (My Father did not have a car but petrol was rationed and it was unlikely that, even if he had he would not have been able to use it. My Grandfather had put his car 'up on blocks' in the tin garage until the war ended).

'The second answer to your question is: 'The Stanford in the Vale job would need transport which would be provided by your firm, should all of you six men desire to undertake that sort of journey each day which is around 33 miles each way from Moreton-in-Marsh which would be your starting and finishing point, with exception of one hour per day travelling expenses paid to you all per day by our firm.

'Is there any more questions? 'Yes, we both said together, both of us intending to ask different questions at the same time. The District Engineer had got the decency to see our anxiety so he took my mates question first. He wanted to know the answer to the question 'what is likely to happen to me or us two should we not decide to take either job but to stay here on this site until the finish'. 'Ha, well yes, a very good question that is'. 'Therefore, my answer to that is you both would be liable for conscription as you both would have to report to the labour exchanges in your area, which, in your cases would be Moreton-in-Marsh. Therefore, when you went and reported to the Labour officer that your work had finished at Pershore aerodrome his immediate reply to that would be: 'Was either of you offered other work elsewhere by your firm' . 'Of course, he would also want to know what your reply to this question would have been'. Yes, Ho, well, then I am afraid I must conscript you back to that firm which is still

based at Moreton. So, therefore, that question fell through for me and my mates because we both would not want to put ourselves to all that bother.

'Now, your question,' says the engineer, pointing to me. 'Well', I says, 'what I would like to know is this. 'Should we decide taking the Stanford in the Vale job, could you enlighten me as to the hours per week we would be expected to work and also would any extra travel payment and so forth be granted if me and my mate agreed to work at Stanford in the Vale.

'Another interesting question' was the District Engineers reply. 'Well now' he started. 'Firstly' I am sorry to tell you that, as the transport which will be used for the journey will have its starting and finishing base at Moreton-in-Marsh, you two (meaning my mate and myself) will still have to make your way to the base from your village of Blockley'. 'Secondly, after you two and your other mates leaves the base on the transport provided you all will become eligible to receive one hours travelling time per day, the same price as your hourly working rate, which should make a difference of around 5 hours per week, as the journey will consist of only five days per week, being as there will not be any Saturday working time at all, that distance from home, but there would be work at Moreton-in-Marsh base should either or anyone care to do it. 'Now, thirdly, and lastly, being as you would be travelling out of your local pay area, (that is of course Gloucestershire, in your two cases). we would be expected to reimburse all of you with the London rate of pay. In your cases that would amount to an extra 2d to 5d.per hour, I would therefore think, it's all food for thought don't you think', was the District Engineers remark. 'Right now', the discretion is yours from now on, I will expect a complete answer from both of you by this time next week when I will be here again and also help you two to make all final arrangements should you decide upon the Stanford in the Vale employment, which I hope, you two will take in preference to the Moreton-in-Marsh site, as that may be drawn to a close any time'. With that speech, the Engineer jumps up and says 'thank you and goodbye' and out of the office door he went.

So, with a move like that, it left my mate and I a little flabbergasted for words for a minute or two until the Site Foreman spoke for the first time throughout the whole procedure. He began by saying things like 'how lucky we two were to have that kind of consideration as regards another job, from the District Engineer. 'He would not do it for some of the other employees on this site including himself'. Now, by this time, with a speech like that and also coming from a chap holding such a position as himself, I began to think at once that he was somewhat becoming jealous of us to some extent and therefore wanted us to go off the site. So, after, he had rattled on for a few more minutes, I together with my mate just thought we had had enough, it was time to stop him in his tracks from throwing out his insinuations and so forth, and bring him to heel a bit, to which we both done just nice and quietly by telling him a few of our home truths about his misbehaviours. After some thought by him, he just quietened down and just dismissed us two accordingly, out of his office, with a reminder that we two was to let him know by Monday morning of our decision as regards taking one or other jobs on another site.

Well, us two made our way back to our living quarters we began to think all sorts of things, concerning our future employment with the Electrical Installations firm. 'Firstly, we began by discussing how much better or poorer, off we would be if we did take the Stanford in the Vale job and so forth.

'Well, our own conditions concerning that job was 'it might be better if us two did decide to join forces with the other four and take the job, or else, we may find ourselves joining the dole queue or be conscripted somewhere else, as the governments powers during the wartime, we would therefore not have cared for that sort of thing to have happened to us. Secondly, we quickly thought that we would be somewhat better off in our pay packets, not by much, as for instance we would have to take all of our meals packed up from home, roughly three meals per day. These things we had not been accustomed to. So, therefore,

it would also put extra strain for purchases on our Mothers to know what to put up for us each day We decided to leave that question unanswered until we had a discussion with our Mother's during our weekend off work.

STANFORD IN THE VALE

My Father and his mate decided to take the work at Stanford in the Vale.

A Taxi from Youngs of Stow-on-the-Wold, a Buick, was hired by the Electrical Installations and picked up my Father and his mates from the Black Bear at Moreton-in-Marsh, My Father told me that 'Tiddley' White, and 'Roy' Parker went with him. The Taxi was driven, fast, by a young man my Father called 'The Cockney Kid'. The Electrical Installations paid my Father and his mates an extra hours pay for travelling one way, they did not get paid for the hour travelling back.

('Tiddley' White and his wife lived at the Railway Crossing on the Fosse Way just above the Darlingscott crossroads. At that time the old railway line was operating and Mrs. White used to open and shut the gates. Passenger Services continued to June, 1929 and freight services until the 1960's. This was originally part of the old Moreton-in-Marsh to Stratford on Avon Tramway.)

'Parker' (his surname was always used) (Evan Roy C. Parker) was a Journeyman Baker for Tarpletts in Paxford before the war and lived at Todenham.

On their drive to Stanford in the Vale they sometimes asked for the driver to stop on the journey at Burford. There was a lady there that made cakes and sold them and a cake made a welcome addition to their lunch boxes. Food was rationed during wartime and my Father's Mother would have been hard pressed to fill his lunchbox, let alone make cakes with the sparse butter and sugar rations. Rations were limited to 8 ounces of Sugar, 4 ounces of Margarine and 2 ounces of butter per person during the War.

On one trip back from their work, the two others in the car asked the driver of the taxi to stop at the Mason's Arms at Fulbrook, My Father, Parker and Tiddley White wanted to get home and an altercation took place. Apparently, Parker picked up a bottle from his lunch bag and was about to (in my Father's words) 'brain' the Cockney Kid. (Hit him over the head). He might surely have killed him. However, Tiddley White (who had been a Police Officer at one time), said, 'Now Roy, Now Roy'. By his actions my Father felt that Tiddley White 'had something 'on' Parker because Parker lowered his arm immediately and the danger was past.

As the work at Stanford in the Vale was drawing to a close and my Father was in danger of being sent to Ireland, he happened to mention to Fred Sandford who was working at Northwick Park, about his problem. Fred, knowing the type of work my Father had done at the brickworks, looking after the machinery, electric motors and equipment, recommended him for the work of looking after the newly built Water Pumping Station and Reservoir at Northwick that served the hospital. My Father went to see the Foreman at the American Army Hospital and was given the job as 'Pump House Attendant' looking after the Water Treatment Works (the Pump House and Reservoir that had just been constructed at Northwick Park to serve American Army Field, 327th Station Hospital in anticipation of D Day. The Hospital later took German privileged prisoners (medical personnel) from 1944 under the International Red Cross. The camp was being constructed by Higgs and Hill of London. Today (2023) company is now called BAM.

And so it was on 20th February, 1943 that my Father left the Electrical Installations and started work *'for the maintenance people at Blockley Hospital Feb. 23, 1943'*. He had to get 'his release' from the Electrical Installations to take up the new position.

(As far as I am aware there are no photographs of the Pumping Station that was situated across from front of the Northwick Mansion, so I have included a sketch below).

NORTHWICK PARK

When my Father started the job at Northwick Park, most of the main buildings including the Pump House (situated across from the Mansion) and the Reservoir, constructed in the lee of Augusta (a wood named after Lady Northwick, Elizabeth Augusta Rushout), had been built. The Reservoir had an upright gauge on the front painted white with black lines and this showed how full (or empty) the reservoir was.

Behind the pump house was a deep covered well where the water was pumped from into the Pumping Station to have chlorine and alum added and the quantity pumped recorded, then on up to the Reservoir. The pipes passed through a pit constructed of the same common semi-engineering bricks as the remainder of the Camp. This pit contained the water meter and also over time attracted a number of frogs and toads.

(On the 1898 Ordnance Survey Map of the site where the Pump House was constructed, 3 wells are shown on the site where the pumping station was built).

At the lower side of the Pump House there was a big brick tank built to take the backwash water and the three sand beds that the backwash water ran through before it seeped back into the ground.

Inside the pump house was the large, round tank filled with filtration media. The pumps and the tanks that fed in the alum and chlorine that was used to treat the water before it went to the reservoir. These pumps were on a timer. However, the Chlorine had to be mixed to the required solution by my Father by tipping out of a big glass carboy into a measuring jug and then adding it to the water in the chlorine tank. This had to be a precise amount as so many parts of chlorine were required in every million gallons. Measurements of the dilution were taken at several points on the Camp and were recorded in a book.

The Pump House had large double doors and a small door was placed, at my Father's request, in the right hand main door that the Pump House Attendant could step into and out of without opening the main doors.

(My Father was living at home at Pitt Cottage when he started this job in 1943. He had to cycle from the cottage to the Pump House. In the 1940's access to Northwick Park from Blockley could be obtained via the main gates and lodges off Park Road (formerly called Hedge Lane). So, my Father cycled to work that way and then walked across the field between the top lake and the ice house to the Pump House. For two years after starting this job he did not have a day off.)

My Father notes that he paid Income Tax up until April, 1944 at 18/- (Eighteen shillings a week). *'PAY AS YOU EARN STARTED FIRST WEEK IN APRIL (1944). ONE DAYS HOLIDAY EASTER SUNDAY WITHOUT PAY. FIRST WEEK OF P.A.Y.E. £1.5.0 Second £1.1.0 Third 15/- FOURTH £1.5.0 FIFTH £1.5.0.'*

THE WORK AT NORTHWICK AMERICAN ARMY HOSPITAL

The hospital at Northwick Park was busy during the war. Of course, a blackout was in place and my Father recalled that in, what was called the 'the covered way' that stretched the length of the camp, with the main operating theatre and hospital wards off. On dark nights, it was only by the 'swish' of the starched dresses that the Nurses wore that he knew they had passed by him. That, and maybe a spoken acknowledgement.

(Picture taken when camp was abandoned and disused around about late 1960's)

Ambulances set off at night to the coast (Southampton) to bring the wounded back, or were sent to meet the hospital trains that came into Moreton-in-Marsh for those who were walking wounded.

The Surgeons operated on all nationalities and initially any limbs that were amputated and the dressings and other items were burned in the boilers in the main Boiler House in one of the three big Robin Hood Major Boilers.

However, one day the ether in the items that came from the operating theatres caused one of the doors of a Robin Hood Major Boiler to explode and it fled across the boiler house. It nearly hit one of the Boilermen. After that a proper incinerator was constructed to take Operation Theatre waste.

There were both American and German Surgeons operating on the site. Harry Bricknell, the Carpenter, had to make one of the German Surgeons a stand to go round the operating table as he would have, otherwise, been too short to reach the table to operate.

The German Surgeons operated during the day and the American Surgeons at night.

BOILER HOUSES

There were two main Boiler Houses. One with the three Robin Hood Major Boilers provided hot water for all the main buildings and wards on the site. Above that there was a Steam Boiler House. The Steam was used for sterilizing instruments for the Operating Theatres and for keeping kitchen equipment clean and sanitised and laundry.

The fuel for the boilers was Coke. (Although it is a different story the British Gas Industry during WW2 converted coal to gas, the by-product of which was Coke that burns at a high temperature and is very efficient. An allied story is that of the small ships, the Collier's that brought the coal from the coalfields during the war and again, allied to that, is the role of women in keeping the gas production going during WW2.)

Around the camp were smaller boiler houses that had to be kept supplied with coke for the smaller Robin Hood or pot stove boilers (of various sizes) there. This meant that the men employed at the central boiler house were also responsible for keeping those boilers fuelled and the water hot at these sites that were bath and wash houses for personnel living on the Camp.

For the Boiler-men, it meant a lot of loading and pushing of heavy metal wheelbarrows full of coke to keep the bunkers full at the main boiler house and all around the camp.

After the Northwick Brickworks closed in 1941, my Grandfather, a lorry driver at Northwick Brickworks and then aged 59, also went to work on stoking the boilers at Northwick Camp until his retirement about 1948.

CONDITIONS ON THE CAMP

My Father records that the Americans took over the Camp *November, 29th 1943, by D.C. R.E.* (This I think stands for Deputy Commander Royal Engineers). When the American staff came to the hospital, there was plenty of food. In fact, my Father told me that the American's were very wasteful. Whole chickens and pieces of beef were thrown away by the cookhouse staff with just a few slices taken off them. My Father, on his rounds of the camp used to remove these from the bins and wash them off and take them home because food for the family was very scarce.

However, as the Atlantic Convoys of British Merchant Ships came under attack by German U Boats on the way from America, my Father said that *'Notices, went up in the Canteens'*, saying *'Eat what you take and only take what you can eat'.*

The big Boiler House was one of the warmest places on the Camp and some of the American Servicemen came into the Boiler House to play 'Craps' in the space behind the big Robin Hood Major boilers. 'Craps' is a game of dice.

My Father was able to take advantage of this opportunity as the American's always had cigarettes and also wanted cigarettes to continue to bet and play Craps.

He was able to obtain some American Tools (including a Signal electric power drill, that I still have and the very large transformer that went with it). Also, as my Father smoked cigarettes then he was able to get a small supply for very little cost.

All meals were provided by the Cook Houses, one of which was situated just across from the Boiler House, so the Stokers were also provided with some food during their shifts.

The German Prisoners, mainly medical personnel, left their mark on the camp by painting pictures on the walls of the canteen situated at the end of the camp just before the old Rickyard (sadly I do not think the items mentioned are there any more). These were beautiful paintings. The main one, on the back wall, was of an Eagle flying above a wild sea and on the left-hand wall a picture of the main Northwick Park with oak trees and some tree fellers working. I cannot remember what the picture was on the right-hand side wall. In the Cinema near the boiler house, there was a picture, that filled the whole wall of a village with roads and people. As these were painted straight on to the brick walls I do not think any of them may have survived, except perhaps the one at the old Cinema that was still standing in 2020.

In latter years Wilmotts from Evesham. a company making spectacle cases occupied some of the huts and provided employment for the Polish people on the camp, particularly the women and girls. For those who want to know more about Polish Resettlement Camps after WW2 there is a link below that was active in 2023.

In later years Dowty's at Ashchurch also provided transport to work for mainly the Polish men. (Dowty's made pit props for mining).

The Cother family who had the Post Office and Grocery Store in Blockley opened a store on the Camp as did Balhatchets, the Butchers from Blockley.

https://www.polishresettlementcampsintheuk.co.uk/northwick06.htm

PART 5

A CHANGE IN CIRCUMSTANCES – MEETING DORA, HIS FUTURE WIFE

During the war the NAAFI at Moreton-in-Marsh RAF Station held dances and men and women from Blockley and villages around attended these dances. This was the place where several men and women in the village met their life partners. My Father was no exception. Thus, it was at a NAAFI dance at Moreton-in-Marsh Aerodrome that my father met his future wife Doris Annie Moore (always called 'Dora').

Dora was an orphan and did not know either of her parents. Her Mother's name was on her birth certificate. The documents held by the Children's Society say that Doris (Dora) was born on 13th March, 1913 at Cookley Farm, High Wood, Eastham and was baptized at Hanley Child Church, Tenbury on 6th April, 1913. to Caroline Annie Moore, age 31. Caroline was employed as a general servant living with her employer, Mrs. Hall, Ashton, Leominster. She earned £12.00 a year.. From writing to the Children's Society I found out from their records that the name of her Father was Andrew Lloyd, age 34, he does not appear on her birth certificate My Mother was christened Doris Annie but throughout her life she was always called 'Dora'. Initially she was was sent to Dinas Orphanage Home for Girls, Brecon at the age of 2 years and 10 months. This was after Caroline's Father, James had died in October, 1915. (I would speculate that it is likely that, while her Father was alive, they had been living on his pension and what Caroline could earn from 'rough domestic work and field work'. (Pensions had been introduced to those over 70 of 'good character' in 1908, five shillings per week) After he died, according to the records kept by the Children's Society, Doris Annie was looked after by two old people for the sum of 2/6d a week but suffered some neglect, so the application was made to place her in a children's home. (An Extract of the document sent to me by the Children's Society is in Part 11 My Mother's Story. Extract from the letter and transcript of my Mother's File Documents held by the Children's Society). Although the document seems to indicate that Andrew Lloyd had died and was buried at Handley Child on 9th December, 1915. I think this was a fabrication as I have not found a Death Certificate for him of that date. However, I have found a Death Certificate that indicates, Andrew Lloyd died while living on a farm in March 1921 and his death was registered at Bromyard. He died of a heart condition in his 40's.

Dora was brought up in two Children's Homes in Wales and one at Altringham in Cheshire. Then, she was moved to a Children's Home in Fareham in Hampshire, where they trained the girls to be housekeepers and go 'into service'. In the 1939 Wartime Census her address was 19 Marius Road, Balham and Tooting Central, Wandsworth, England. She told me she was working 'in Service' as a housemaid/housekeeper for a Doctor and his wife and left there to join the NAAFI.

I gather at times the Doctor's wife, who was an alcoholic did not treat her very well. She almost 'brained' my Mother over the head with a bottle one day, and Mother almost suffered a nervous breakdown from working there and she told me that she was very happy to join the NAAFI 'to better herself'.

(From early 1941, it became compulsory for women aged between 18 and 60 to register for war work. Conscription of women began in December. Unmarried 'mobile' women between the ages of 20 and 30 were called up and given a choice between joining the services or working in industry. When the NAAFI started recruiting for the war, she joined at the age of 29 and was sent to Innsworth Lane, near Gloucester to train as a storekeeper. Her first posting was as Assistant Storekeeper at Moreton-in-Marsh. She always spoke affectionately of the Storekeeper in charge at Moreton, a Scotsman. I never did learn his real name but she always referred to him as 'Jock'.)

The woman who was in charge of the NAAFI also took her under her wing, and although I was told her name, I cannot recall it. I think she found companionship with the other girls – sometimes they used to be able to get a ride on Johncey's Coal Lorry into Moreton but my Mother was also renowned for the speed at which she walked into Moreton from the Aerodrome on various errands.

(I gather that there was a large girl in the NAAFI called Alma and she had a bit of bother getting up on to the back of Johncey's Coal Lorry, so the men used to be quite happy to help her up!).

My Father used to go to the dances held at the NAAFI with a number of girls from Blockley and they cycled to Moreton-in-Marsh. The girls treated him, being a bit older, as something of a chaperone. Ruby Newbury who was courting his brother, John, who was with the Gloucester Regiment in India, also used to go with them.

Iris Diamond, one of my Mother and Father's friends from the NAAFI.

The girls in the NAAFI were quite 'adventurous' and they used to turn the hands of the clock back. (Dances were supposed to end at midnight). Father often found himself cycling back to Blockley in the early hours of the morning.

One night, my Father did not realise that this had happened until he was cycling up the hill (or rather pushing his bicycle up Bourton on the Hill road by Bourton Hill House and the Church Clock struck 2.00 a.m.). The local Policeman had just called at Bourton on the Hill House to 'leave a card to say he had called' as the Police did in those days. The Policeman said to him *'Late tonight, Ernie'* and they stopped and had a cigarette together.

My Father rode his bicycle quite fast down 'Blockley Hill' (which my Father always called 'The Cross' because, once a medieval cross was said to stand near the entrance to Hailstone Farm), into the Village and one night he nearly ran over the Village Policeman, Troughton, walking up the hill, with his bicycle, in his dark clothes and cape. It was moonlight and in wartime, there were regulations for lights on vehicles, including bicycles. Obviously, vehicles including cycles could not go without lights but bicycle lights had to be dimmed and pointed downwards and only an inch wide beam was allowed. My Father was travelling as he put it with his grey raincoat on and a flat cap. On the way down the hill, as it was moonlight, my Father saw the Policeman but the Policeman did not see him and started pushing his bicycle across my Father's path resulting in a very narrow miss as my Father sped past him. The Policeman shouted but Father kept going.

Later, in the Royal Oak Public House that night, the Policeman came in with the story of nearly being run over by someone on a bicycle on Blockley Hill (The Cross). He told the landlady, Mrs. Hodgkins, 'I know who it is and I shall 'have him'. He wears a grey raincoat'. However, he went on to say who it was and it was not my Father who was standing next to him! Of course, when the other person was challenged and later told my Father all about it, he had a perfect alibi, as he was at home asleep at the time with his wife and children.

Another close shave my Father had while riding the bicycle down this hill was a rabbit ran across the road and got caught by the front wheel and the mudguard. Father managed to stop before he was thrown off and the rabbit ran away minus some fur from its back.

My Father's girlfriend, Dora, was welcomed into the home at Blockley by my Grandparents. My Grandmother, having lost her own daughter became very fond of my Mother. As a consequence, Dora was a frequent visitor to my Grandparents home whenever she could get time off work in the NAAFI. At the end of the war when my Grandfather put his car back on the road he used to pick her up from Moreton-in-Marsh to bring her over to the cottage at Blockley.

I know that my Father wrote frequent letters to my Mother during the years before their marriage in 1947. Sadly, none of these now exist. Although in my early years they were kept in a box at our house, 6 Mill Row, and always started with the affectionate 'Dear Ducksie', that was my Father's pet name for my Mother. (My Father's brother, John, got married early in 1944 to Ruby Newbury and bought and moved into the Old Bakery, in Bourton on the Hill).

Knowing that the Lodges at Northwick Park were vacant. My Father approached Captain Churchill and asked if he could be granted the tenancy. Captain Churchill had known my Father for many years, since his time of working at the Brickworks as a young man, and was happy to give the tenancy of the Lodges to my Father on the proviso that they would open and shut the gates to let his guests through. So, my Father and Mother and Grandmother got to work making the Lodges habitable.

The Lodges were very convenient for my Father's work . The Pump House situated in front of Northwick Mansion was just a short walk across the field from the Lodges and 'the Camp' situated in the field at the other side of the Mansion House.

The woman in charge of the NAAFI had said she would give Dora a Wedding Tea when she got married but in the end this did not work out as the lady was left a Post Office Stores in the south of England by one of her relatives and left the NAAFI before Dora. Consequently, my Grandmother prepared a small tea at Blockley.

My Father and Mother married at St. Peter and St. Paul's Church, Blockley on the 3lst May, 1947.

My Father's brother, John, was their Best Man. 3lst May, was a Saturday and they walked to the Church in their best suits. (The Villagers who met them on the way thought they were going to a football match – either the Villa or West Bromwich Albion in Birmingham). Daisy, who had married George Hicks, one of my Father's Brothers was at the wedding, as was Ruby, married to John Hicks. (Both my Father's Brothers). Daisy and Ruby, mischievously, made what is called an Apple Pie Bed at the Lodges where my parents were going to live. (An 'apple pie bed' is when one of the sheets is folded back on itself so if you get in you cannot stretch your legs out. Consequently, the bed has to be remade before you can get into it).

There were no pictures of the Wedding as far as I am aware. But below is a picture of Ernie and Dora taken at Broadwell in 1945 before their marriage. They used to walk to Broadwell to visit a friend of Dora's, who I believe was called Charlotte Bisley, and who had also been in the NAAFI. Charlotte lived on the Estate owned by Lord Ashton of Hyde, Broadwell Hill

There is a break in my Father's diary writing and this is, likely, because he was newly married and adjusting to his change in circumstances. I am reliant on the information that I wrote down from our conversations.

My Father married at the end of May, 1947 and they were very happy at The Lodges. The heavy horses, then kept in the Park, Beauty, Bowler, Bounce and Blackie, used to come up and rub themselves against the gates making them rattle. My Mother used to 'make a fuss of them'. Rabbits were able to get under the floorboards of the lodges from the outside and they could be heard scuttling about. There were some gypsies camped near the Park and one night one of them stuck their head into my Mother and Father's bedroom window in the early hours of the morning and frightened them. My Father shouted and the person ran off.

The Lodges were situated both sides of the road that led from Park Road to the Mansion with the decorative iron gates between. On the left-hand side going down was the kitchen and wash-house and living area and on the right-hand side the bedroom. My Father used to carry my mother across the road at night when they were going to bed and one night when he was doing this some people were walking down the road. My Mother said, 'put me down', put me down'. He did and she ran into the Lodge on the bedroom side blushing.

They were both very happy at the Lodges, had cleared and planted the garden and had wood for the fire and had settled in. My Father had also become established in his job and was now employed in his capacity of Pump House Attendant by the Ministry of Works that had taken over from the War Department. On 5th June, 1948, he was now part of the Government Establishment.

I am not sure why they moved from the Lodges but I think it was because, Captain Churchill wanted them back. However, my Father was offered 6 Mill Row a largish house down by the Northwick Sawmills. It was occupied at the time by the Estate's Manager, Conrad Warner who was moving out to another Estate House at Sleepy Hollow opposite the Old Silk Mill.

My Mother and Father hired Gordon James (who had a couple of lorries, at that time. Gordon was in the wood trade and his lorries were in a Green livery but later he became the main haulier for Northwick Brick and Tile Works, later, after it was sold, Northcot Brick and Tile Works. He changed the livery to Red later). He moved as my Father said 'our few sticks of furniture' to their new address at 6 Mill Row but, to my Father's regret, he could not move the ton of coal that they had just had delivered. I am not sure how that dilemma was settled but I am sure that my Father would not have left it there and my Grandfather may have helped to move it later.

My Father told me, the Warner family were slow in moving out and my Father and Mother were moving their furniture and chattels in through the front door as the Warners were moving theirs out of the back door!

ANOTHER DIFFICULT TRANSITION

Around about July, 1948 my Mother became pregnant with her first (and only) child (me) at the age of 36.

Bearing in mind that my Father had lost his Sister when she was expecting a child, my Mother's pregnancy must have caused both my Grandmother and Father some concern. I know that my Mother was supported by my Grandmother and they spent a lot of time together at this time.

The National Health Service had just been introduced, on 6th July, 1948 and my Mother, as a Prima Gravida (Older Mother) was to have her child at the newly built Sunnyside Maternity Home in Cheltenham. (I do not think it was an easy birth and in those days the conditions would have been 'regimental'!). Before the advent of the NHS (National Health Service) a home birth with midwives cost one shilling and sixpence!!

There was debate at the time whether expectant Mothers should be given pain relief and the following appeared in The Lancet at around that time:

('Newspapers even published strident demands from women demanding pain relief. A letter published in the *Gloucestershire Echo* in 1942 and signed by "Six Expectant Mothers" complained that "any Cheltonian, rich enough to pay for [pain relief] can have it", but the "poorer class" were "damned". The war had changed their expectations. They protested the fact that:

"If a man wants a tooth out he has to have gas or cocaine. A soldier on the battlefield, when in great pain, has morphia administered to him. But a poor woman in the throes of childbirth; what does she get? Queen Victoria had her whiff of analgesics for all her confinements and what is good enough for Queen Victoria is good enough for SIX EXPECTANT MOTHERS OF CHELTENHAM.")'

However, my Mother was destined to spend a lot of time during her pregnancy with my Grandmother as at some time in early Autumn, 1948, my Father's disability concerning his right hip became painful and acute. One morning he was in so much pain with his 'gammy' leg he could not get out of bed.

One of our local Doctors, Dr. Jean Haine, who was in partnership with her husband Dr. Frank Haine, was called to see my Father. She diagnosed arthrodesis of the hip and arranged for an appointment to be made for him at The Wingfield-Morris Orthopaedic Hospital in Oxford. The Hospital still exists but now goes under the name of the Nuffield Orthopaedic Centre.

I am not sure how my Father got there, but initially after being seen by several Doctors there he was going to be turned away, as it was thought that nothing could be done. However, at that time Professor Foley was heading up the team of Surgeons and he said to his team 'Now that this man has come all this way, surely we can do something for him'.

(It is possible that my Father benefited from the work of Professor Girdlestone who in 1943 described an Orthopaedic procedure that was intended to rescue hip joints in humans. The procedure (Femoral head ostectomy also known as a Femoral head and neck ostectomy is a salvage procedure, mostly used in cases of severe damage through hip dysplasia or Arthritis in which the head (and sometimes the Neck) of the Femur are removed allowing fibrous tissue to grow in place, creating effectively a pseudo-joint).

However, my Father's procedure was more complicated in that 2 inches of bone was taken from the shin at the front of his good left leg and fused into the hip of his right hip. This procedure lengthened the leg by 2" leaving a 2" deficit that required the sole and heel of the right boot to be built up by the two inches. The operation also stiffened the hip and as a result my Father was never able to ride a bicycle again.

The result of the operation was that my Father spent a long time (over 6 months) in the Wingfield Hospital flat on his back in a full plaster . However, had my Father not had this operation that, in terms of the surgery of the day, was a success, he would have been in a wheelchair for the rest of his life from the age of 37, as it was he had an active life and died at the age of 94.

It was also fortunate that the National Assistance Act, 1948 had brought in free health care for all as my Father and his family would have been unable to pay for an operation of that magnitude.

Obviously, being in hospital for a long time flat on his back waiting for the grafted hip to heal, he built a good rapport with the Nursing Staff as he could not do anything for himself except his arms were free and he could feed himself. Every other bodily activity had to be carried out by the nursing staff. My Father was attended by a male orderly and what my Father called 'Tow' was used to wipe his bottom.

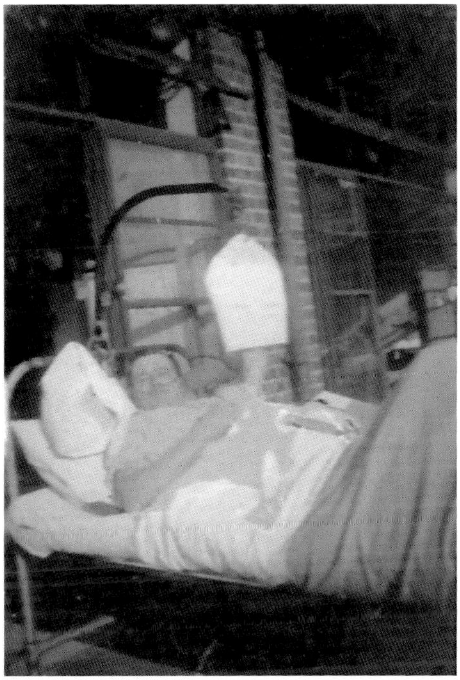

I have a picture of my Father on the balcony of the Wingfield Morris Hospital as during the summer beds were pushed out into the fresh air.

My Father became friends with some of the Nurses and in particular, Joan Skeet. She was a follower of The Oxford Cheetahs a British Speedway motorcycle team founded in 1939. During 1948 and after renovations to the track in 1949 the Cheetahs were beginning to get back to racing. She also used to 'smuggle in' cigarettes for my Father. (He was still a smoker at this time and the cigarettes were likely either Woodbines or Senior Service). I was named Joan after her and along with my Mothers Picture my Father carried Joan Skeet's picture in his wallet for the rest of his life.

Photograph of Joan Skeet that my Father carried in his wallet.

My Father recalls that the first time he was allowed to sit up to get out of bed, he could not because of vertigo, postural dizziness because he had been prone in bed for so long. Eventually, he was able to get up with two physiotherapists (Orderleys he called them) and begin to learn to walk again between parallel bars. Although the first time he did this they had to lay him down quickly because of vertigo again.

I know that he frequently wrote to my Mother, Dora, as he used to use her 'pet name' 'Ducksie' as the salutation, but sadly these letters have not survived. My Mother and Grandmother also visited him at the Wingfield hospital and hired a taxi from the Village to do so. My Father was in hospital for the latter part of my Mother's pregnancy and I know she spent a lot of time with my Grandmother during this time. I know my Father had returned home, (to my Grandparents home), by the time of my birth.

My Mother was in Sunnyside Maternity Home in Cheltenham awaiting my arrival. In those days they kept Mothers in hospital for at least 10 days following the birth of a baby, particularly older Mothers and my Mother was just 37 years of age when she gave birth to me.

My Father did come to visit at the Sunnyside Maternity Home after I was born and he struggled up three flights of stairs on crutches. Endearingly, as I had red hair he referred to me as a 'little Tamworth' (a piglet that is covered in red hair)!!

I do not know how my Mother and Father managed financially during this time.

My Father had started his Government Service on 23rd February, 1943 and on 5th June, 1948 he started his Established Service with the Ministry of Works. I believe that as an established employee my Father may have been paid sick pay by the Ministry of Works. (It is recorded in Hansard in 1952 that a Major Lloyd asked the Financial Secretary to the Treasury what had been the total cost of the industrial paid sick leave scheme operated in certain Government establishments since 1948. His question was answered by Mr. Boyd-Carpenter who advised the scheme covered 56 Departments, some of which did not maintain complete records of sick leave. In the circumstances, he said, he did not think the cost in clerical manpower of a special inquiry into the cost would be justified 'at the present time').

I am certain that my Father, as he was frugal with his money, would have had some savings and that his Mother and Father would have helped in any way they could.

So, my Father returned home from hospital and lived at 6 Mill Row, Blockley. However, my Father's spell in hospital was about to be augmented and I am afraid I was the cause.

Apparently. a few months after my birth my Mother put me in my Pram out in the fresh air just down the garden path. I began to cry and so my Father went to pick me up and comfort me. Unfortunately, he tripped up on the wooden garden edging and broke his good leg where the bone had been removed for his hip. The consequence of this accident was that he ended up in the Wingfield again with his leg in plaster for another 3 months. During this time, my Mother again, spent a lot of time with her Mother in Law at Pitt Cottage.

There is a gap in my Father's records of water pumped from the Pump House between December, 1948 to 6th November, 1949 and reason for this probably equates to his time spent away from home in hospital and regaining some fitness before his return to work.

PART 6

THE 1950's

BACK TO WORK

I am sure that the Ministry of Works would have been keen to get my Father back to work as soon as they could after his operation. As a result of the operation he could no longer ride a bicycle and so had to walk to work through the Park from 6 Mill Row, Station Road, in all weathers. Apart from the snow and ice in winter, one of the other perils of the walk was that the milking cows in the park used to lie on the tarmacked road because it was warmer than the fields and early mornings when it was a thick fog 'when you could not see a hand in front of your face' my Father had to avoid tripping over them. Often it was only their breathing that alerted him to their presence.

I cannot remember my Father having any time off for illness during my childhood. He was always conscientious and reliable. He certainly did not want any allowance made, by others, for his disability.

He always soled and heeled his own boots and I still have the Cobblers anvil in my shed at this time (2023). He had to be careful not to slip and always carried a long stick with him with a square metal end, that he called 'a paddle'. On days off and other days he always used a normal walking stick.

My Father worked solely as the attendant at the Pump House until March 17th 1951. He was told by Mr. Rice, who was the Site Engineer for the Ministry of Works at the time, on the 16th March, 1951, that he had got to do other work besides the Pump House and would be working at the Boiler House on the Camp stoking boilers 9 a.m. to 4 p.m. the next day. Effectively this meant that my Father was being asked to do two jobs and his written record notes that he had raised this issue with Mr. Rice and the Union Representative. The note in his General Note Book reads: *'April 3.51. 3 Water tests made readings as follows: main cookhouse 0.4 p.p.m, 30 abulution 0.3 p.p.m. 118 ablution 0.4.1/2 p.p.m. Mr. Rice and the Union representative came up to Pump House told him about doing two jobs, it's now in their hands.' (p.p.m means parts per million (of chlorine in the water).* However, as my Father goes on working both jobs with little time off, I can only assume that nothing was done about his circumstances at that time.

The work he was doing as Pump House Attendant was for the most part lighter than the work that he did as a Stoker at the Boiler house. However, one only has to read his book of General Notes at this time to see that the work at the pump house, maintaining the pumping machinery and equipment there, measuring the chlorine into the chlorine tanks that injected the water with so many parts per million via poppet valves and carrying out the appropriate measurements, required thought and attention to detail combined with the ability to maintain the electric pumps and other machinery.

There were occasions that he had to carry heavy items at the pump house including the large glass carboys packed in straw in metal frames containing chlorine that he used to add to the water in so many parts per million.

The chlorine then had to be added to the tanks. My Father had a measuring jug to do this as it had to be measured accurately. He then recorded the measurements at several points on the camp of the amount of chlorine, in so many parts per million, in the water.

Of course, he had to walk from the Boiler House on the camp to carry out work at the Pump House and also carry out physical checks to the reservoir, again in all weathers. This could sometimes be twice a day or more often if there were problems as well as the walk to and from work. This walk was not always on the concrete road to the Pump House or the tarmacked road to the Camp. He often had to walk up across the field to the Reservoir that stood above the camp in front of the wood called Augusta. Sometimes, if he visited the pump house on his way to the camp he took a short cut across the field from the main drive to Northwick House to the Pump House in front of the mansion.

On one occasion the Northwick Estate had a black Aberdeen Angus Bull and this was put in the Reservoir field that my Father had to walk through. Instead, he took an alternative route and walked along the road at the back of the Northwick Gardens and through a little shrubbery by the Orangery and out across the field in front of the Mansion. He had to go up to the Reservoir, however, and got there by going into Augustus and over the fence on to the top of the Reservoir. Looking out across to the Camp he noticed that Harry 'Yatty' Beasley (who lived at Sedgecombe Farm had been cornered by the Bull. Harry was 'doing a dance' around the big Oak Trees there to avoid it. My Father managed to divert the Bull's attention long enough so that Harry could join him on the top of the Reservoir. 'Close one Harry, he said!' to a grateful Harry.

An entry in his notebook dated Mar: 17, 1951 reads: 'Started working on Robin Hood Major Boilers and doing pump house work as well, a lot of walking it means me doing".

He also had to walk all around the Camp with full barrows of coke for the Ablution Huts that were spread around the camp and the smaller boilers there had to be stoked at least once a day.

In his notes of 28th April, 1951, he records that coke had not been delivered and they are burning coal dust on boilers again. The coke was delivered on 1st May, 1951.

There are notes in the General Notebook about Polish coke being withdrawn.1954. (The Polish refugees at the National Assistance Board hostel at Northwick had been allowed an allocation of coke for the pot stoves in their huts. By the entry, I take it that the government, or the Site Manager, Mr. Juni, had decided to withdraw this concession. It would have meant that the polish refugees would have had to pay for their own fuel).

In all, the work was heavy and physically active. It is testament to my Father's stoicism and personal strength and determination that he was able to do this work.

An entry for April, 13th 1951 notes: *'Working on boilers, Mr. Rice brought time clock, he says everyone must clock on even building workers. Chlorine tank changed'.*

My Father was also asked to work lengths of time without relief and so on September 1st 1951, the entry reads; *'A Relief done Pump House and Boilers, First Saturday off for 5 weeks.'*

FAMILY LIFE AT 6 MILL ROW, BLOCKLEY

The Post War WW2 period was difficult in that food rationing did not end until mid-night on 3rd July, 1954 when I was just over 5 years old and at School at the Church of England Blockley Girls and Infants School in School Lane.

Meat was one of the last items to be taken off ration. The Conservative Government who returned to power in 1951 on a manifesto that urged an end to rationing as they sought to portray the wartime post war Socialist Government as incompetent.

I am sure that the post war years were difficult for my Mother and Father. Any savings my Father may have had would have diminished during his time in hospital and he had a wife and child to support.

At that time, the house we lived in at 6 Mill Row, Station Road, Blockley, rented, from the Northwick Estate, did not have any electricity and I can remember the gas lights being lit on the wall in the kitchen.

At that time the kitchen also had an 'open coal (or wood) fired range' on which as well as providing heat for the room you could also cook on. This room was always very warm and it was not until later years that my parents used 'the front room'.

There was also a 'back place' with a Belfast sink and a bricked in copper boiler in the corner. The 'back place', was brick built, with an uninsulated corrugated tin roof. I think I was about 4 years old when the copper boiler was taken out of the 'back place' and the open range removed from the kitchen and an ordinary coal fired fireplace installed with a brick surround and electric lights put in by the Northwick Estate. After that my Mother and Father bought a gas stove as a gas meter had been installed in the 'back place', where the old copper boiler had been, and my Mother cooked on that. A clothes mangle stood

Mill Row. 6 Mill Row far right. Northwick Estate Houses built 1837

in the corner by the back door to wring out the washing from the wash tub on Monday mornings. My Mother always wore a big red rubber smelling apron that almost came down to her feet, for washday Mondays and the 'back place' used to fill with steam.

There was an open fire with an iron surround in the front room but until the alterations had taken place we did not use the Front Room at all. Both of the main rooms of the house downstairs were quite large but there was no bathroom and we used to have a big tin bath in front of the fire in the front room. My Father and Mother had to carry buckets of hot water from the 'back place' to the tin bath that was put in front of the front room fire. There was a really sturdy iron guard in front of the fire attached to the wall to stop me from touching the fire and getting burnt.

However, one night as I was lying on my tummy in front of the fire reading a book a spark came out of the fire and through the guard and landed on the back of my leg just at the back of the knee. My Father noticing this told me not to fold my leg but of course I did and the spark burnt above and below the back of my knee. However, my Father seemed to know all about wounds like this and applied immediate first aid but I still carry the scars from that spark on the back of my right knee to this day.

(Northwick Timber Yard was just over the bridge over Blockley Brook by the Mill Pond and my Father used to go and get and carry up a long tree branch to our house. He brought it through the front door and stretched along the Sitting Room and through the corridor to the Kitchen. He used to saw logs off this for the kitchen fire. This used to save money on paying for coal for the fire).

On really cold winter nights I used to like having ice from the water butt outside to cool the water in the bath and to play with as I sat in the bath. Unfortunately, my Mother and Father noticed that the ice burnt my fingers so that pleasure had to stop.

My Father's parents, my Grandparents, always played an important part in my Father's life and that of my Mother. My Mother went to my Grandmothers on Tuesday's and Thursdays. My Grandmother did not like shopping, so my Mother did it for her. In fact, unless in Grandfather's car she did not venture out down the street and only occasionally walked down to the garden. (At that time there were many shops in Blockley village, including a Co-op. My Mother's Co-op number was 6338 and my Grandmothers 7284. Mr. Oliver was the Co-op Manager at the time).

I spent a lot of time with my Grandparents. Although I could never have replaced her, I am sure I reminded my Grandmother of her own daughter, who she lost at the age of 20. I was often told I was, 'like Lizzie'. Before I went to school, during the hunting season, they followed the Heythrop and North Cotswold Hunts as my Grandfather knew the ground well and also most of the men and women that went hunting or followed the hunt as they were contemporaries of his. As hunting takes place in the Autumn and Winter I was bundled into a blanket on the back seat of the car and we had home cured bacon or sometimes tasty cheese sandwiches and a flask of hot tea. One day, at Tangley Wood between Icomb and Rissington a fox was killed and my Grandfather picked me up and ran down the field so that the Hunt Master could 'blood me' (smear blood on my cheeks from the fox). I did not consider this awful or horrible, it was part of the way of the life of a country child. I got the foxes tail to take home and it hung in the cottage at Blockley until it just disintegrated with time sometime in my teenage years.

After WW1 my Grandfather had been a lorry driver driving the Scammell at Northwick Brickworks and always drove with the window of the cab down. The same applied to when he drove the car, so the blankets and coats were essential to keep warm.

My Grandmother made lovely food, bone stews, pastries and cakes. When I started school, instead of going to St. George's Hall for school meals like the other children, I walked up to my Grandmother's for a hot lunch. This saved my Mother from paying for my School meals which at that time I think were 6d. a day but the price rose to a 1/-d. by the end of the 1950's. On Tuesdays and Thursdays I was met outside the school by my Mother and we walked up to Grandmothers together.

My Grandmother made all my skirts, blouses and dresses at this time.

When I was born my Father gave up smoking. He had been a heavy smoker of both cigarettes and pipe tobacco. In later years he said he gave up smoking because he could not afford the cost of tobacco and me. If that is the case, the second benefit was that with the money he saved from smoking, in 1956, he was able to buy a black and white television set from Eagles of Moreton-in-Marsh. There were limited channels in those days and I cannot say that I remember watching it very much. What I do remember is sitting at the table with my Father some evenings after tea and learning my times tables and doing mathematics with cowrie shells and steel washers. We also listened to a lot of radio and I have particularly fond memories of Listen with Mother with my Mother, Children's Hour between 5.00 and 6.00 p.m. (Particularly the Eagle of the Ninth) and The Archers at quarter to seven. If my Father was working an early or a late shift, I used to sit on his lap or the cabinet next to the wireless and listen to the radio with him. I remember being so sad when in the Archer's programme. Grace Archer, Phillip Archer's then wife, (Grace Fairbrother before her marriage to Phil) died in a stable fire trying to rescue her horse Midnight.

I did not want for toys. Apart from a green and brown felt Bambi that my Father made for me while he was in hospital, my very first doll that I called 'Fatty' was made of old brown lisle stockings, stuffed with more brown lisle stockings and tied at the neck with a face drawn on it in biro. I loved that doll and had it with me until it fell apart in the early 1970's. My Father made me a Dolls House with electric lights run from a battery and switched on using real switches and he made the furniture. He also made a cot for my dolls. My Grandmother always bought me lovely books for my Birthdays and Christmas including Green Willow Farm, that I really loved and still have today. My Mother would have bought them for her from Miss Stenning's Newsagents (then called the Paper-shop) in the village. One Christmas, I had a lovely Rosebud Doll given me. My Mother had made all the clothes for it and the same year my Father had made a cot for it and my Mother made the mattress, pillows and pillow cases, sheets and blanket and knitted a small quilt that I still have. Now in my early 70's, I gave the doll and the dolls cot away to a child in the village called Cloe Spencer in 2021. I made a new set of bedding for the cot including mattress and pillow.

Mrs. Brooks who lived across the road at Rock Bank made me both a gollywog and a bear. The bear was 2 ft. high and made out of a grey blanket. My parents gave these away to other children when I left home. I also had a conventional bear that was bought for me by my Mother and I still have that bear.

My Mother also won a 'walking doll' for me at Moreton-in-Marsh Autumn Fair about 1956. I had this doll for a number of years but when my parents moved to Pitt Cottage, Blockley after my Grandfather died, they kept it under their bed and unfortunately a Queen Wasp got in and made her nest in the Doll. So, sadly, it had to be removed and thrown away.

A picture of me and my, then new Rosebud Doll in the 1950's and a picture of the same doll, 70 years later in the cot that my Father made for her in 1953. Pictures below:

We did not have a bathroom at 6 Mill Row, nor an indoor toilet. The toilet was the other side of the stream across a little bridge and initially was a vault toilet that needed to be cleaned out when the vault got full and buried on what we called 'The Miskin'. It was a big vault at the back of the toilets and I only remember it being cleaned out once. In the mid 1950's, around about the same time as they took out the gas lighting, the fireplace range and the old 'coppers' from the houses, the Northwick Estate installed Elsan Pan toilets which had to be emptied by my Father and the occupants of the other properties and buried on 'The Miskin' when they became full. This was fairly frequently (probably once a month). There was also a lovely Lilac Tree growing at the side of 'The Miskin'. 'The Miskin' was also situated next to the Mill Pond at what used to be called 'The Bone Mill; but was when I was small, the timber yard for the Northwick Estate. The big circular saw was run by the turbine using the power of the water in the mill pond. All the men who worked there my Father knew well and I was particularly happy to talk to Tom Box. Tom had been a friend of my Father for many years since their days working at Northwick Brick and Tile Works before the war. My Father used to relate that when he was courting his wife, Tom used to cycle to Leicester on a bicycle with one handlebar.

Picture of me and my then 'new' Doll in the 1950's, about 1953.

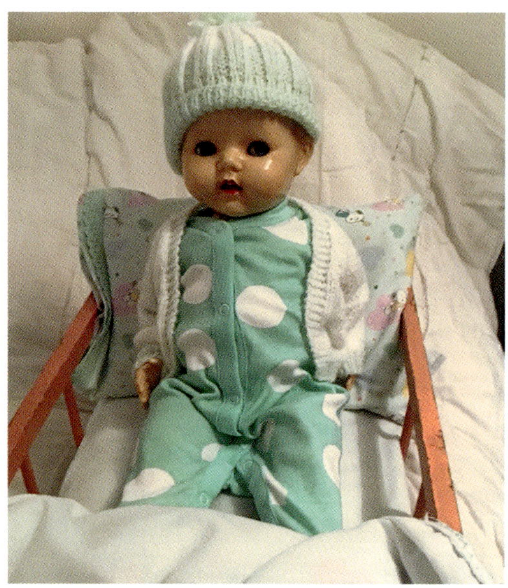

Picture of the same doll when I gave it away, some 70 years later, lying in the wooden cot my Father made for it.

I also used to like playing in the sandpit that was by the side of the road at the Timber Mill. Harry Eastbury, who used to think he was in charge of the Timber Mill told my Father that I could not play there. However, my Father saw Captain Churchill and he said, I could play, there. So, I went on happily making sandcastles with my bucket and spade in the sandpit.

In those days there were also a lot of water voles living in the banks of the stream. My Father used to grow all the produce for our kitchen on the garden there and onc year he found that the Voles had eaten out the middle of several of the cabbages he had grown by the brook. The cabbage looked fine and healthy until they were pulled up for the table and cut open and there was no inside to them at all.

We also kept chickens in a fowl pen at the side of the road by the timber yard. Jack Turvey the farmer at Northwick Mill did not keep down the rats in the 'bowsing' where he kept his store cattle and sometimes pigs. Our fowl roosts were then visited by rats that stole the eggs and of course were dangerous to health. I can remember my Father spreading a brown coloured poison on pieces of bread to set in a safe place away from the chickens for the rats to eat and also my Mother became adept at 'snolping' (hitting it with a heavy stick to kill it) any rat that got caught in the then 'gin' traps my Father set. 'Gin traps were not illegal then' . My Mother did not like doing this but she did it to protect the chickens. The word 'snolp' does not appear to be in the English Dictionary but it may be an old English country word or may be borrowed from elsewhere. 'Bowsing' I think is a synonym for 'house', so in this instance it was a place for 'housing' cattle.

I was also given a small piece of garden of my own to cultivate and with my Father's supervision was shown how to grow, firstly easy things, like radish and beetroot and potatoes and then more difficult to grow vegetables, like carrots, peas, cabbage and beans and then flowers like Sweet Williams and Godetias.

My Father also taught me to read and write and my tables and how to do 'sums' before I started school at 5 years old. I knew my tables up to and including twelve times table. To work out numbers for mathematics we used to use metal washers and cowrie shells to add and subtract. I wish I could say that this was appreciated when I got to School because I had 'done' all the cards at the front of the teachers table on the first day (sums and words and sentences). However, despite my Father's requests I was held back in this first 'infants' class and made to read 'Dick and Jane' even though it was too easy for me.

Similarly, and I don't know how she came to learn it, my Mother taught me all about wild plants and trees and she used to bowl me along in my 'push chair' on long walks around the area in the afternoon and point out and name plants and trees as we went along. Then, if we came back through Draycott, I was rewarded with a pink ice cream on a stick from the shop in Draycott.

I also remember one occasion when my Father, Mother and me were out walking and at the Draycott turn, a Lyons Maid Ice Cream Van came along and my Father stopped it and bought us ice creams. We sat under the high wall at the edge of the field on the right on bales of straw to eat them. This was a one off and never happened again.

I was most fortunate in that I had a lovely childhood with people who loved me very much.

I do not think that there was any money to spare in the household. My Mother was very careful with her housekeeping money and I never remember her buying herself new clothes. My Father felt that well-fitting shoes were most important and we were all well shod with good fitting shoes that in my younger days were bought from Wheatley's in Moreton-in-Marsh, where Enid Taylor from Blockley village worked. Underclothes were purchased from the Co-op in Chipping Norton and my Grandfather took my Mother, Grandmother and me there in his car. He never came shopping with us and neither did my Father. I was about 4 years old when I 'christened' the floor of the Co-op. (I peed on the floor). Quickly my Grandmother found a duster and mopped it quickly and pushed the wet duster under the bottom of the glass fronted counter!!).

MY FATHER'S WORKING LIFE DURING THE 1950's

The Camp at Northwick housing the Polish Refugees was at its maximum capacity during the 1950's until the mid 1960's and it was essential that a good supply of water was available and the Robin Hood Boilers in the main Boiler House and in satellite boiler houses around the camp serving ablutions, were operating at maximum capacity.

My Father worked a shift pattern. 2 p.m. to 10 p.m., 10 a.m. to 4 p.m. and 6.00 a.m. to 4.00 p.m. Later, a 10 to 6 night shift was also worked at the Boiler House. The Site Engineer employed by the Ministry of Works and responsible for other sites, at Springhill, Moreton-in-Marsh and Rissington was Tom Rice. There are references in my Father's records to the times when a Time Clock was first introduced and everyone had to clock on and off and then, in time, a reference that the Time Clock was replaced by one from Spring Hill. (Spring Hill Camp was a German Prisoner of War Camp constructed opposite the Campden Cross Roads to Seven Wells/Snowshill) An entry for March 21st 1952 reads "working at pump house and coke trimming. Mr. Rice informed us that a new type of time sheet will be in working progress from Mon 24th"

My Father was a conscientious worker and took pride in the accuracy of his work. In those days looking after the Water Pumping Station was time consuming and required diligence and accuracy, both of looking after all the equipment and recording the water used. Chlorine had to be measured by hand and tipped from the carboys into a jug and introduced to two tanks fitted with poppit valves that injected the mixture into the water supply. Regular readings were taken at various sites on the Camp, for example the cookhouse, the wards and the ablutions of the parts per million of chlorine in the water and complaints were made if it was too high or too low.

My Father hated it when the Relief Attendant had to be used to cover holidays at the pump house. (My Father was only off sick with influenza once, in all the time he worked at the Camp). Most of the men employed on Father's days off, apart from Mario, one of the Polish Refugees who was also employed by the Ministry of Works, did not like the pump house work and could not be relied on to perform their duties neither well, nor accurately.

Equally, some of them were also lazy and did not do their fair share of the work at the Boiler House. Loading coke into wheel barrows from the compound to the bunker in the Boiler House was one particular job that one or two of my Father's mates tried to shirk. This left one or other of the Stoker's following them to work twice as hard both to stoke the boilers and bring in coke for the bunkers. The men who were working, stoking, with my Father in the early 1950's were: W. Humphries, Harry Franklin, Tommy Cross, Tommy Hopkins and Maurice Eastbury (all local men).

There is an entry for Friday April, 17th 1952 that reads: 'Robin Hood Major Boilers working 24 hours continuous firing from tonight and Pumps running'. This may be because the camp was now running at capacity with the number of Polish Refugees housed there.

My Father was also responsible for supplying the meter readings for the Northwick Mansion. Because their old water supply (halfway down left side of the reservoir field) was sometimes uncertain, Captain Churchill had decided to connect the Mansion to the Camp supply. This was the first time that chlorinated water had been supplied to the Mansion and the Cook soon complained about the chlorinated water turning her potatoes 'black' while in the cold water waiting for cooking.

The supply to the mansion had been problematic for some time. One of the main reasons being that the cover was ill maintained and the occasional cow fell through it. This obviously contaminated the supply. (My Father was responsible for alerting Con Warner the Estate Manager of this problem at least twice).

During the 1950's because of his technical ability, my Father, not only did his own job looking after the Pump House and Stoking at the Boiler House, he also helped out the 'Fitters' that came on to the camp to install and change the pot stoves in the Nissen Huts and on March 14th 1957 'Assisted Electrician with ladders tightening up Line taps from No. 106 to 82. On Monday, March 18th 'Mr Bailey died this morning at Cheltenham Hospital'. Mr. Bailey had been in charge of the Sewage Works and I believe he fell off the high wall at the side of the sewage treatment tanks near the Camp at Northwick.. On Tuesday, March 19th 1957: T. Hopkins away sick, that only leaves two of us to do all the work'.

THE BENEFITS OF WORKING AT THE PUMP HOUSE

When my Father was at the Pump House he worked on his own and my Mother frequently walked from 6 Mill Row to the pump house and took me on visits there before I went to school and after, during holidays and weekends. We played ball in the grounds. One day I had a small green ball, that I loved, with fishes on it and we were throwing it to each other. I missed the ball and it fell over the small wall that was next to the road in front of the pump house. Although we looked and looked we never ever found that ball again. It was as if it had disappeared into thin air. I know my Father looked for it for years afterwards.

If we walked up with my Father through the Rickyard. Blackie, one of the heavy horses, used to wait for my Father at the gate. My Father used to put me on his back and little legs astride I hung on to his mane and he walked alongside Father to the Pump House gate where I was lifted down and Blackie got a reward.

He also took me to see the Grass Snakes a'frogging at the Bathing Pool below the Viaduct that Lord Northwick had built in 1873 on the road from Blockley to Broad Campden. I was told to sit quietly on the grassy bank not far from the Sweet Chestnut Tree (no longer there) and watch. Similarly, we watched rats stealing eggs from the

Chicken Houses in the Rickyard (they rolled them down the chicken ramps tucked between their jaws and their front paws).

My Mother and Father used to sit on the concrete step outside the Pump House and watch the changing formations in the clouds. There was a large expanse of sky that could be seen from there towards Cadley and Brailes Clump to the East and Ilmington and beyond to the North East. The Mansion and the hill to the left of it and trees blocked the view of direct North.

The long lake (that previously had been used for skating by Lord Northwick's guests. Their cars used to be parked alongside the lake with the lights on at night while they skated), now had 3 islands built in it. These islands and the Willow and other trees planted on them and general neglect of the lake had led to a lot of reeds and trees growing in the lake bed. In the evenings 'murmurations' of Starlings coming into roost could be seen. The bundle of these birds twisted and turned rapidly in the air making exotic patterns before suddenly landing all at once in the trees and bushes on the lake.

As I became older, my Father explained what the equipment in the Pump House was for and how he maintained it. I also used to go and read the meter that registered the amount of water being pumped to the Reservoir built on the bank under the wood called Augusta for him. I loved doing this as there were also frogs and toads that got into the damp space in the pit there.

I only saw the 'back wash' in operation once. The water came out into the big tank below the Pump House and then when my Father turned the wheel in the outlet to the tank, the water flowed into the three sand filled filtration beds in the Pump House grounds.

THE BOILER HOUSE

As the years went by and supervision of the site by the Site Engineer became intermittent, we also went up to the Boiler House once and later twice a week to enjoy lovely hot baths in the bathroom that was there.

As I got older I used to walk up to the Boiler House to walk back home with him through the Park to Mill Row. Sometimes, we would meet Captain Churchill and my Father would stand in lengthy conversation with him. As I grew up, (aged about 7), I was bought a second hand green bicycle, this replaced a blue trike that I had. I am afraid I could sometimes be a naughty child and used to have what my Father called 'a paddy') if something did not go right for me. When I was given the green bicycle, I had been used to the stability of 3 wheels on my trike, so learning to balance on 2 wheels was somewhat difficult. (My parents were walking to the Pump House and I was supposed to ride my bike along the smooth tarmacked park road to follow them). Just starting off from the back door I wobbled and fell off, started to 'have a paddy' and cry and threw the bicycle it into the side of the waterbutt that stood at the corner of the house. My Father did no more than say 'Come on, Mother' to my Mother, and they just walked off. Two minutes later, I was on the bike pedalling fast up behind them!!!).

PART 7

THE 1960's, ONWARDS AND ANOTHER CHANGE OF CIRCUMSTANCES

In 1968, I had married Keith Joseph Fell and moved to Scotland and so was no longer living at home. July of 1968 was the last time I saw my Grandfather and Grandmother together, as they both stood in the road outside the cottage and I hugged them and they waved me goodbye.

RENOVATIONS OF AND MOVE TO PITT COTTAGE

My Grandfather died on 6th February, 1969 at East View in Stow on the Wold. Sadly, in his later years, he was suffering from dementia as he fell and hit his head at the Russell Spring in the village while collecting water (he may have had a transient systemic attack then. TIA). After my Grandmother fell and broke her hip helping him, he had to be transferred to East View in Stow on the Wold to be cared for.

Probate was proved on 10th April and he left £2,219.00 which paid for his funeral and other expenses involved with the Estate.

By May, 1969 my Father was spending money buying materials and renovating Pitt Cottage in Blockley so that they could move in and look after my Grandmother. When my Grandmother came out of hospital she moved in with my parents at 6 Mill Row until the work at Pitt Cottage could be completed and my parents and my Grandmother could move there.

At this time Pitt Cottage had no indoor toilet or bathroom and the interior was in some disrepair as the floor boards, were rotten and the cottage damp. My Father had to find, a not inconsiderable amount of money, at that time, to make changes and alterations to the house so that they could move there to live.

My Father records that he paid Mr. E. Barrett, Builder and Decorator, the sum of £564.00 for alterations to the cottage on 20th January, 1970. This was for 7 sheets of 3 ft.×2 ft.6 inch Plaster Board and 4 cwts of gravel and one domestic bath, given in discount for the sum of £564.00 as above.

He paid Maurice Davies the sum of £41.1s and 11d. for rewiring the property and an additional sum to Barrett of £56.17s.6d. for sink unit and concreting the front room floor, 12th March, 1970. He also paid a Mr. Newton for drawing up plans and presenting them to the Council the sum of £5.10s.0d.

The rest of the work to the Cottage was done between my Father and my Uncle John.

The Bond Motor car was hard worked at this time, bringing slabs from the Camp at Northwick Park to be put down in the dirt yard at the cottage and for other work. When the Pump House finally stopped being used at some time in 1971, after he had already been relocated to Moreton-in-Marsh Fire College, my Father brought one of the chlorine tanks home and cut it in half to make plant boxes. I have these in my yard today (2023) and Graham Stayt a local builder (related to the Hicks Family by his Great Aunt's marriage to Joseph Hicks, one of my Grandfather's brothers) made stands for them.

I do not have detailed Diaries written by my Father from this time. It is possible he was far to busy to write a detailed Diary. However, he did keep copy letters and details from that time and they now form part of this narrative.

On the 27th March, 1971 my Father sent the undernoted letter (copy below) to Con Warner, the Estate Bailiff terminating the tenancy of 6 Mill Row. My Grandmother, Mother and Father then moved into Pitt Cottage after its renovation.

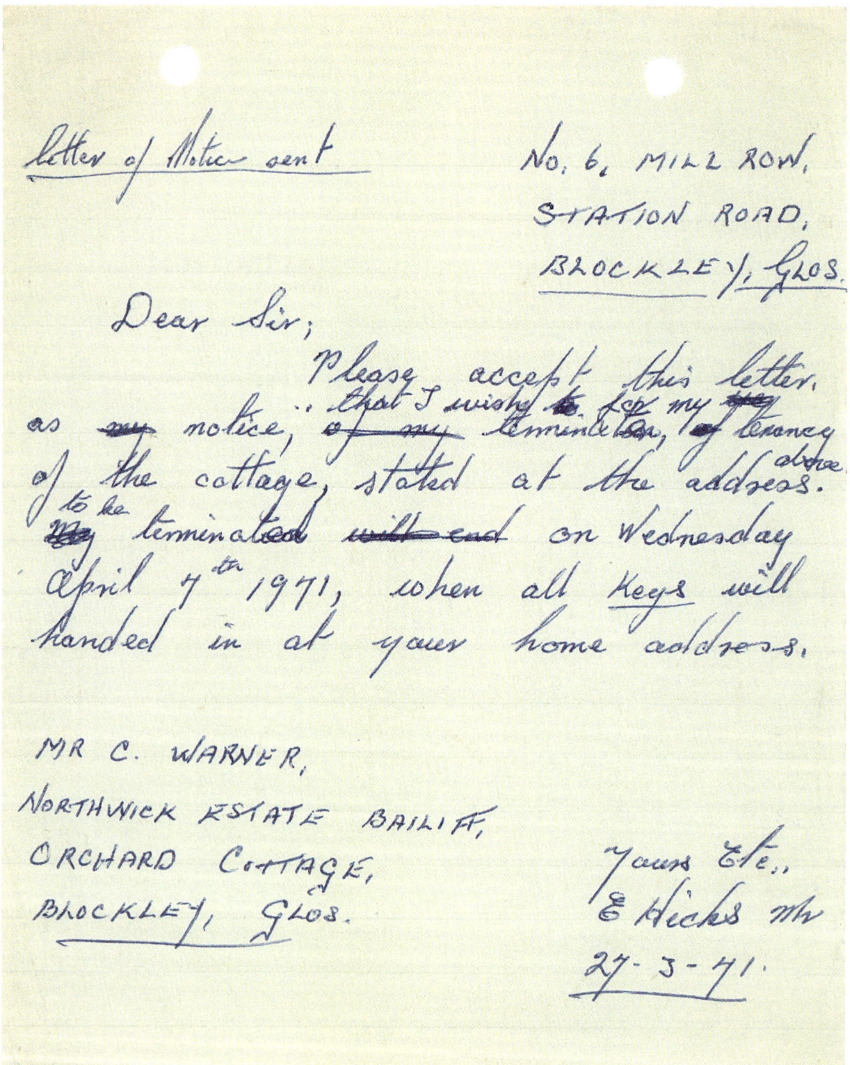

letter of Notice sent

No. 6, MILL ROW,
STATION ROAD,
BLOCKLEY, GLOS.

Dear Sir;

Please accept this letter, as notice, that I wish for my tenancy of the cottage, stated at the above address, to be terminated on Wednesday April 7th 1971, when all Keys will handed in at your home address.

MR C. WARNER,
NORTHWICK ESTATE BAILIFF,
ORCHARD COTTAGE,
BLOCKLEY, GLOS.

Yours Etc.,
E Hicks mr
27-3-71.

Copy of letter written to terminate tenancy of 6 Mill Row, Station Road, Blockley

PART 8

TRANSITION FROM NORTHWICK PARK NAB HOSTEL TO MORETON-IN-MARSH FIRE SERVICE COLLEGE

My Father had worked at Northwick Park looking after the Pumping Station and Stoking boilers since the early 1940's. Between 1949 and 1960 the National Assistance Board Hostel for Polish Refugees was operating at maximum capacity. However, from the 1960's onwards, as the people housed in these camps were beginning to settle, many moved out the of the camps in search of better work and accommodation. Some emigrated to other, then, Commonwealth Countries, Australia, New Zealand, Canada, for example.

Those that remained in this area were moved to Council Accommodation in Lower Quinton, some went to Aston Magna and others moved to Evesham. Some joined together and bought a hotel somewhere in the North of England.

Across the country, as people moved out, the camps closed. By the mid 1960's there were just a handful of people left at Northwick and it was closed in 1970 when the last family was moved out to Stover Park, Newton Abbott, Devon.

This would have been an uncertain time for my Father. He had no transport of his own and although he was an 'Established employee', he could be offered employment anywhere in the Country by the, then, Ministry of Public Building and Works and it would be up to him whether he accepted it or not.

My Father must have written a letter to the Ministry of Public Building and Works asking for clarification of when the Polish Hostel was going to close as I have a reply to this letter, which he kept, as over.

During this period the Site Engineer employed by the Ministry was Maurice Davis. A local man born in Stow on the Wold, Maurice had site responsibility for Northwick Park Polish Hostel, Moreton-in-Marsh Fire College, Great Rissington Aerodrome and was also 'cleared' to work at GCHQ in Cheltenham.

My Father and Maurice had a good rapport and I am sure it is as a result of this that my Father was eventually offered employment at The Fire Service College in Moreton-in-Marsh, setting up the instruments for the fires and carrying out other electrical work required on that site. My Father's attention to detail was ideal for this sort of appointment. I do not think this would have happened had 'Tom Rice' still been the Site Engineer for the Ministry of Public Building and Works.

The other bonus was that as Maurice Davis was a qualified Electrician. He often did other private jobs in the area, as he was building his own house in Hospital Road, Moreton-in-Marsh at the time (subsequently called Oak House) and needed all the

Depot Superintendent,
MINISTRY OF
PUBLIC BUILDING AND WORKS
R.A.F. Station,
Little Rissington,
Cheltenham, Glos.
Telephone: Bourton-on-the-Water 606 Ext 244.

Our reference: 2204/3 3rd March, 1970.
Your reference:

Dear Mr. Hicks.

Polish Hostel - Northwick Park

With reference to your letter of 28th February it is advised that to date we have no definite information on the closure of the above site. As soon as we have a firm date for closure the merits of your case will be taken into consideration and treated in accordance with present Department policy.

Yours sincerely,

R. Taylor,
for Depot Superintendent,

money he could scrape together. As a result my Father worked with him as his 'electricians mate' and they rewired several churches, quite a few private houses and other electrical work in the area.

Maurice was also responsible for referring my Father to the Ministry of Public Building and Works for the Imperial Service Medal for my Father's long service through various Ministries.

The letter that my Father wrote in 1973 is as under and his service was confirmed and the medal awarded on my Father's Retirement from the Service in 1978.

(Note: The Fire service had taken over RAF Moreton-in-Marsh and renamed it the Home Office Fire Training Centre. In 1966 The Home Secretary announced the re-launch as the Fire Service Technical College to provide a world class establishment for the training of firefighters that would last long into the future. It was officially opened by Her Majesty Queen Elizabeth II on 17th May, 1974.

No. 1. Pitt Cottage
High Street, Blockley
Nr Moreton-in-Marsh
Glos. GL56 9HF

To Whom This may Concern;

I have had the misfortune to have lost my Establishment Documentary Record, - containing the Established number of years service with the War Department, and other Ministries, since my entry into Government Employment.

I started my Employment with the War Department on February 23rd 1943, - and became Established in 1952. As it was appropriate before 1949 - half a year of service was retained by the Ministries, - therefore on becoming established in 1952 I had standing to my credit, - for those Established years service about 6 years and some odd days.

On my supplying this information; would it be appropriate, or in accordance, for me to be supplied with a new, and up todate, document of my Established recorded years.

Yours Faithfully
E. Hicks (Mr)
Auxiliary Electrical Worker
Department of the Environment
March 2nd 1973.

By 1976 the work to build the college was complete including the planting of 80,000 trees and in 1981 when the Senior Staff College in Dorking closed the College became the home of training for senior members of the UK Fire Service.).

MORETON-IN-MARSH FIRE SERVICE COLLEGE

When my Father was transferred to Moreton-in-Marsh Fire College, one or two of the workers for the Ministry of Public Building and Works considered that my Father with his disability should not have the job. As a result they put him through unauthorised 'tests'. One of his new colleagues thought he could not climb up the iron rungs of the ladder that went up the side of the concrete 'ship; that they use for some of the fire exercises at Moreton. (The Fire College has a ship, lock and lagoon for training). However, if this person expected my Father to fail 'the Test' they had imposed on him, they were sorely disappointed. (These iron rungs do not need to be used to access 'the ship' as there are access stairs with handrails to get inside). My Father also set up and calibrated the instruments for fire training.

Despite my Father being over sixty, he would never have allowed or shown his disability to 'get the better of him' and so without more ado climbed up the ladder.

(Evidently, they did not know that many years ago when at the Northwick Brick and Tile Works he had been one of the lads that had been told off for climbing up the ladder that the steeple-jack had been using to maintain the Hoffman Kiln Chimney (for which the lads were soundly told off by the Foreman and told never to do it again).

I know that my Father regretted leaving Northwick and particularly the Water Pumping Station that he had looked after for 35 years since its construction in 1943.

My Father did go back to the Pump House as by then the camp was empty and John Spittle a local farmer from Sheaf House Farm in Blockley was keeping his milking cows on the old Camp in some of the huts there and needed a clean water supply for them. My Father taught John (and his Brother Pat) how to carry out the work at the Pump House and make sure that he was up to the appropriate standard.

The letter he sent to the Spittle Brothers terminating his involvement is hereunder. The original is very damaged so I have copied it:

No.1 Pitt Cottage
High Street,
Blockley,
Moreton-in-Marsh, Glos

Spittle Bros
Sheaf House Farm
Blockley

Dear Sirs,
I am writing to say that I wish to discontinue my twice weekly visits to the Pump House at Northwick on October, 30th 1971.

On September 16th 1971, I was in contact with Mr. C. Warner concerning the treatment of all water pumped since September, 12th, 1971, when all the chlorination plant failed to work any longer, due to age, I told him the responsibility was his for all untreated water pumped to the Northwick House.

Mr. Warner's reply was that, new water mains were to be installed within the next week or ten days of my interview with him.

Up to the time of me writing this letter, 'Sirs' I find nothing has been done as regards getting treated water to your milking parlour, and Northwick House, 'therefore, think, the discontinuance of my visits to the Pump House are appropriate.

Should I not see either of you, Sirs, before the above mentioned date, I will leave the keys to the pump house on my last visit, at your milking parlour.

The maintenance which is needed, is the winding up of the time clocks, (weekly) the greasing of water pumps on every visit, with the expectation of the tubular heaters being kept switched on during cold, frosty conditions.

Yours, etc.,
E. Hicks

Quite rightly, my Father did not want to be responsible for untreated water being provided to either Northwick House or the Spittle's Milking Parlour on the Camp.

TRANSPORT

Until 1961 my Father had walked everywhere, to and from work and at work and we relied on, what was then, a good bus service, run by Rouse's the local bus company who operated from their garage in the village of Blockley. All of Rouse's drivers were local and known to my Father. Ernie Compton, Dennis and George Rouse, and Harvey Pearson, who used to call me 'Tuppence'.

When we didn't travel on the bus, before 1963 my Grandfather was available with his car to take us where-ever we wanted to go, usually shopping to Chipping Norton or Stratford on Avon.

On the 6th May, 1961 my Father purchased a new 1960 Model Bond Minicar Mk.F saloon. Registration No. 269 DWP and it was delivered taxed and insured for £362. 15s. 0d. This had been altered to hand controls for my Father and a solenoid had been fitted so that my Father did not have to get inside the bonnet and kick start the engine.

Uncle John took my Father out so that he could get used to it prior to passing his test. My Father passed his test at first attempt and from that day on he drove this car to and from work until he was transferred to work at the Fire College at Moreton-in-Marsh, I believe in 1971. In those days, 'Works' Transport was provided by the Home Office and my Father went to work and came back on this. He was picked up and dropped at the Bus Shelter at Blockley that is a quarter of a mile from Pitt Cottage. Bill Sabin from Moreton-in-Marsh used to drive the big green Ministry bus that picked up workers for the Fire College, including domestic staff.

By 1974 the Bond Car was 14 years old and given that Works Transport was provided by the Ministry, my Father decided not to purchase another car and to give up driving. This decision may also have been influenced by the fact that he had spent, what was then, a considerable amount of money renovating Pitt Cottage and that there was further work to do after moving in.

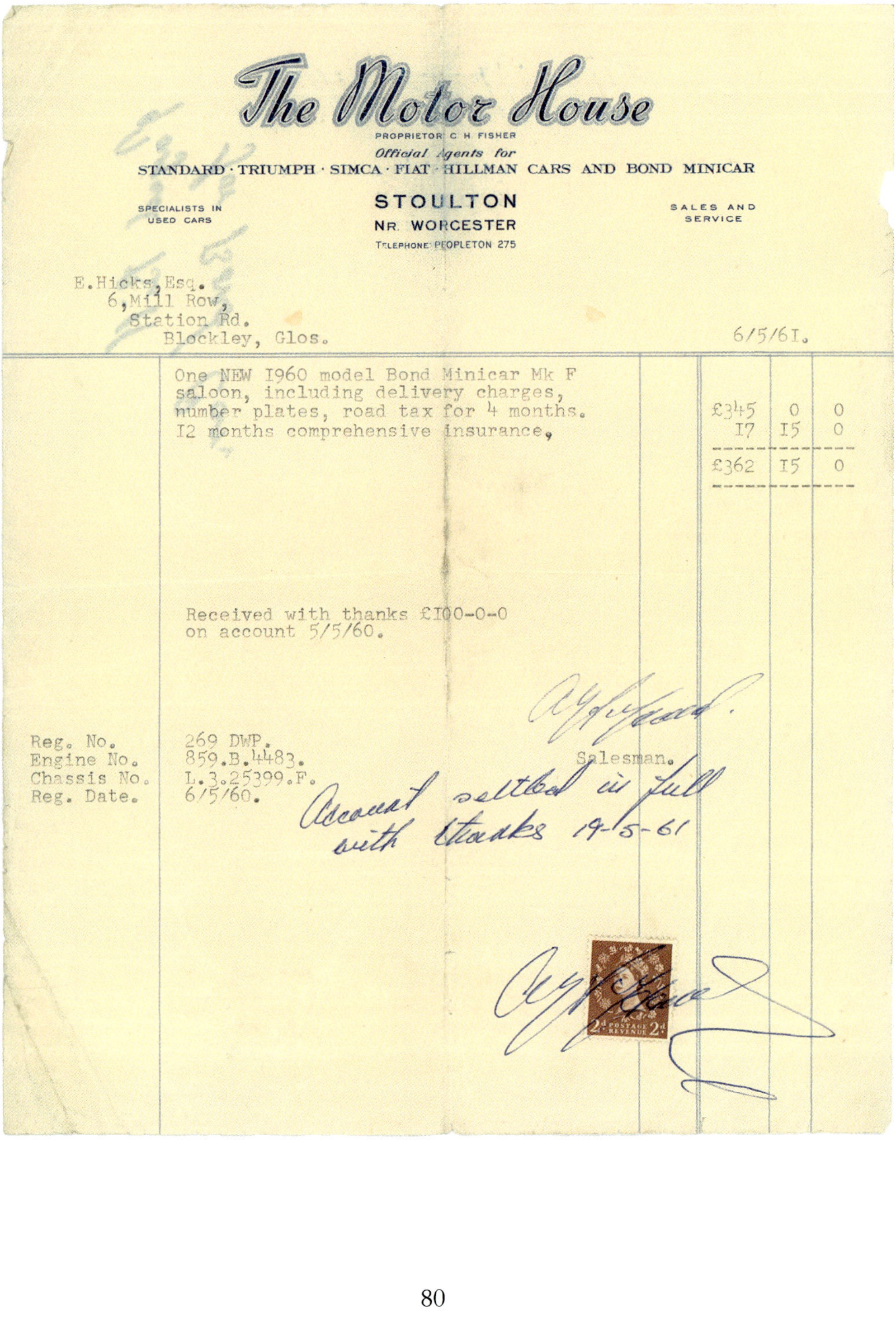

The Motor House

PROPRIETOR C. H. FISHER

Official Agents for

STANDARD · TRIUMPH · SIMCA · FIAT · HILLMAN CARS AND BOND MINICAR

SPECIALISTS IN USED CARS

STOULTON

NR. WORCESTER

TELEPHONE: PEOPLETON 275

SALES AND SERVICE

E.Hicks,Esq.
6,Mill Row,
Station Rd.
Blockley, Glos.

6/5/6I.

One NEW I960 model Bond Minicar Mk F saloon, including delivery charges, number plates, road tax for 4 months.	£345	0	0
I2 months comprehensive insurance,	I7	I5	0
	£362	I5	0

Received with thanks £I00-0-0
on account 5/5/60.

Salesman.

Reg. No.	269 DWP.
Engine No.	859.B.4483.
Chassis No.	L.3.25399.F.
Reg. Date.	6/5/60.

Account settled in full
with thanks 19-5-61

2d POSTAGE REVENUE 2d

My Father sent a letter to the DVLA saying that he no longer wished to drive dated 30th April, 1974.

No. 1. Pitt Cottage
High Street
Blockley
Nr Moreton-in-Marsh
Glos, GL56 9HF.

To Whom This Concerns.

Having received the driving licence renewal form which you sent to me, I would like to say, for your records & information, that I no longer wish to renew my driving licence as I now do not own a vehicle whatsoever.

Yours Etc
E. Hicks Mr
30-4-74.

PART 9

RETIREMENT

My Father retired from work on the 21st October, 1977. A copy of his letter to the Paymaster of the Department of the Environment is shown here.

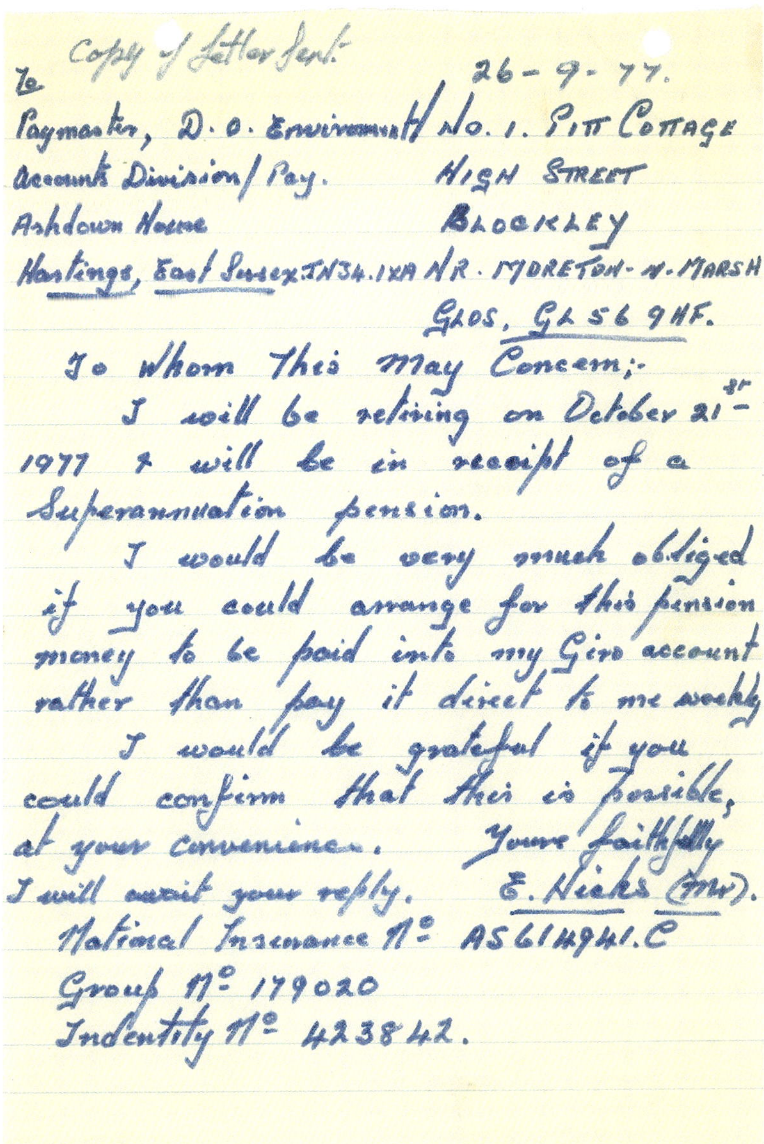

Copy of letter sent

To 26-9-77.

Paymaster, D.O. Environment / No. 1. Pitt Cottage
Accounts Division/Pay. HIGH STREET
Ashdown House BLOCKLEY
Hastings, East Sussex TN34.1XA NR. MORETON-IN-MARSH
GLOS, GL56 9HF.

To Whom This May Concern;-

I will be retiring on October 21st 1977 & will be in receipt of a Superannuation pension.

I would be very much obliged if you could arrange for this pension money to be paid into my Giro account rather than pay it direct to me weekly.

I would be grateful if you could confirm that this is possible, at your convenience.

I will await your reply.

Yours faithfully
E. Hicks (Mr).

National Insurance No AS614941.C
Group No 179020
Indentity No 423842.

The initial months of my Father's retirement from his employment were hard for him.

Retirement meant leaving his work and his work colleagues behind at Moreton and I believe that my Father became quite depressed. However, he was always stoical and never one for dwelling on things very long, so, he took to carving out a new life for himself. Making useful items in his shed, repairing electrical appliances, accompanying Maurice Davies if he had a particular job where he needed assistance, working in his garden (purchased by my Grand-father in 1946 from George Sharp the then village post-man, 100 yards down the road). I think the garden provided my Father (and Mother) with a lot of satisfaction although it was hard work. All watering had to be done by hand from water butts or the brook.

By the time my parents moved back to Pitt Cottage in 1971, with my Grand-mother, she was 87 years of age and becoming increasingly frail and my parents, particularly my Mother, looked after her until the end of her life.

On 17th January, 1978 my Father was awarded the Imperial Service Medal in recognition for his service to The Crown since the early 1940's. Entry below in Government and Transport World. My Father made the frame that surrounds the certificate.

NMENT AND TRANSPORT WORLD, JUNE 1978 3

ISM AWARDS

P. H. V. Badman, 61, RAF Fairford
R. A. Bright, 65, Bovington
W. G. Brand, 61, Dundee
W. E. Cash, 65, Innsworth
E. V. Chisholm, 61, Chatham
C. D. Clements, 62, London
A. Elliott, 65, Catterick
W. Farrimond, 65, Farnborough East
E. A. J. Fizgerald, 65, Bordon
A. E. Freeman, 65, Bulford
G. D. M. Gregor, 64, Edinburgh
D. W. Gray, 64, Aldergrove
T. G. Hall, 63, Driffield
A. Headleand, Bulford
R. Heald, 65, Sheffield
E. Hicks, 65, Moreton-in-the-Marsh
F. J. Holloway, 65, Winchester
F. W. Jones, 63, Brize Norton
G. L. C. Jones, 65, Boscombe Down
J. E Kelly, 58, Manchester
T. T. Lees, 60, Redford
F. G. C. Lewis, 60, Manorbier Camp
D. Main, 63, Lossiemouth
G. K. E. Marsh, 61, Old Sarum
W. E. W. Matson, 63, Montgomery Lines
A. McCorquodale, 63, Old Kilpatrick
M. C. Muir, 60, Greenock
W. K. Murray, 60, Edinburgh
I. J. S. Nichills, 65, Culdrose
T. R. Phillips, 63, Manorbier Camp
Mrs R. A. Pridge, 65, Ruislip
C. C. Radburn, 49, Worcester
E. Radford, 61, Nottingham
D. W. Renshaw, 65, Finningley
J. O. Russell, 59, Edinburgh
A. A. Ruth, 64, Bovington
G. F. R. Seers, 61, Hounslow
P. Scargill, 61, Manchester
J. R. F. Shepherd, 60, Medway
T. J. Shreeve, 63, Manchester
R. F. Sleaford, 56, Cranwell
A. Smith, 65, Camberley
G. J. Spiers, 64, Greatworth
A. Stelling, 65, Ripon
H. G. Stephen, 64, Aberdeen
D. Thomsett, 64, Borden
A. G. Westbrook, 65, Hounslow
C. W. Tatum, 60, Devonport
A. D. Whiting, 64, Portsmouth
A. E. Worsdell, 55, Durrington

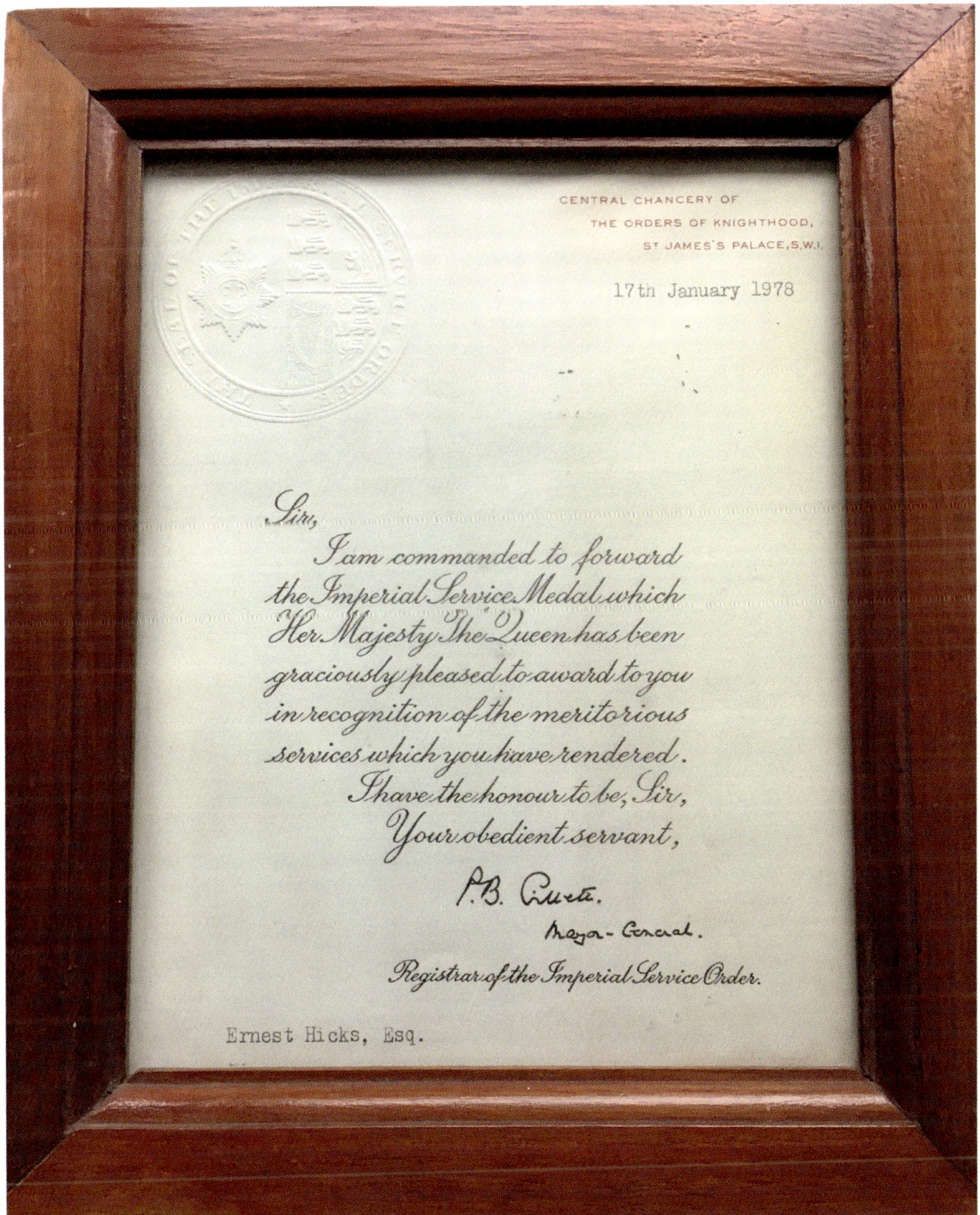

CENTRAL CHANCERY OF
THE ORDERS OF KNIGHTHOOD,
ST JAMES'S PALACE, S.W.1.

17th January 1978

Sir,

I am commanded to forward the Imperial Service Medal which Her Majesty The Queen has been graciously pleased to award to you in recognition of the meritorious services which you have rendered.

I have the honour to be, Sir,
Your obedient servant,

P.B. Gillett.
Major-General.
Registrar of the Imperial Service Order.

Ernest Hicks, Esq.

HIS MOTHER'S DEATH

My Grandmother died on Friday, 10th March, 1978, aged 94, at Moreton-in-Marsh Hospital and my Father has recorded all the steps he took in a notebook. He records that his Brother, John, rang to say that 'he would go to the hospital and see to Gran's belongings and then be over later this afternoon'. (As my Father did not have any transport himself and Uncle John did).

My Father was always meticulous in writing events down. Don Keyte, the Undertaker from Paxford, called on the Friday at 10.30 a.m. to make arrangements for the Funeral and make arrangements for an entry to be put in the Evesham Journal.

My Father rang me that day to tell me that, as his note says, 'her Granny had died at 4.30 a.m on Friday morning. He notes that the message was phoned through to me at 7.20 a.m.

The notes in his book indicate the times that he rang every member of the family and that they had acknowledged the calls. My Grandmother had a Church Service and my Father has also noted that he checked the protocol of the order in which family walked behind the coffin.

The entry in the local Evesham Journal is as under:

Mrs Annie Hicks, of 1 Pitt Cottage, High Street, Blockley who has died in Moreton-in-Marsh Hospital, aged 94, had lived at Blockley for nearly 60 years. Born at Great Rissington on the last day of 1883 she was a daughter of Mr and Mrs Thomas Willett. In 1903 she was married at Great Rissington church to Mr Jack Hicks, of Icomb and they moved to live at Blockley in 1919. Until her husband's death in 1969 she was a keen follower of both the North Cotswold and Heythrop hunts. She is survived by four sons.

The funeral at Blockley church was followed by interment at Blockley old cemetery.

Family mourners included: Mr W. J. Hicks, Mr G. T. Hicks, Mr and Mrs E. Hicks, Mr and Mrs A. J. Hicks (sons and daughters-in-law), Mrs Phylis Jordan, Mr and Mrs Fell, Mr Colin Hicks (grandchildren).

When my Grandfather, John 'Jack' Hicks died, the cottage at Blockley passed to my Father. That was the wish of both my Grandfather and Grandmother.

From what my Father told me, my Grandfather's oldest son, William, had expected the cottage to be left to him, as the oldest. However, that was not my Grandparents wish, as he had left home 'under a cloud' by running away with Agnes Cecile Mayo, a married lady with 2 children, who she left behind, in or around the late 1920's. Probably about 1928 when William came back from India. He had joined the Oxford and Buckingham Light Infantry around 1923 because of lack of work in the area. Before that he had been employed as a hand-maker at Aston Magna Brickworks. (Aston Magna Brickworks was started in 1905 by Lord Redesdale to provide employment for the men in the area). (Construction of Northwick Brickworks did not start until 1924/5). Agnes and William stayed together for the rest of their lives. Agnes died in 1966 and William married Hilda Cyphus in 1970 and lived in Bourton on the Water.

Uncle George was settled in a tied cottage at Daylesford and after WW2, Uncle John had married Ruby Newbury and purchased his own house 'The Old Bakery' at Bourton on the Hill.

My Father, through circumstance, had been the one to stay at home for much of his life and had always looked after his parents, just as they had looked after him in his younger days. My Mother was of the same mind as, not knowing her own parents and my Grandmother losing her only daughter in 1928 at the age of 20, she had adopted my Grandmother as her own. I too had a strong bond with my Grandparents.

By the end of 1977, for various reasons, I had returned to live near Bristol with my husband and after the death of my Grandmother, for the next few years and after our onward move to Gittisham in Devon in 1979, my parents visited and stayed with us and my Father was able to assist in making pens, chicken runs and lots of other items to help my husband and myself with his work as a Gamekeeper on an Estate there.

PART 10
EPILOGUE

1980's ONWARDS

My Father picked up writing a diary again in 1980. He was never one to be idle and if he was not working in his garden between Archway Cottage and Spindlebrook, he was working in his shed at Pitt Cottage using his skills to make Fowl Roosts, Breadboards from timber he had collected from Beech Trees at the Northwick Estate (when several had been cut down in the 1950's), and in 1981 he made me an Oak Blanket Box. (The Oak came from office furniture sent to the Fire College to be burnt and brought home by my Father). It has a metal label (made and inscribed by him) on the inside saying it was made for me (my married name was Mrs. Fell). In addition, he was always available when neighbours needed any assistance and our local Doctor (Frank Haines, who kept bees) used to bring his 'honey spinner' for repair on several occasions. My Father, was competent at woodwork, including dovetail joints, metalwork, electrical equipment, engineering and anything to do with engines. He did all this work in his workshop at Pitt Cottage (in what had been my Grandfather's old Garage where he kept the Ford 8 h.p. motor) in between visiting myself and my husband who was Gamekeeper on an Estate at Gittisham in Devon. He made pens and dog kennels and did all sorts of work to make life easier for us. By this time, he (and my Mother) also had the added worry of my circumstances as by 1984, my husband and myself had decided to go our separate ways.

My Mother, too, was unstinting in her efforts to support and assist me in any way she could and when I returned home to live, sacrificed much of her own time for my benefit. She was always supportive, kind and loving. We all went to see Neil Diamond at the NEC in 1984 and also The Caine Mutiny Court Martial starring Charlton Heston in 1985

The first entries in my Father's Diary for 1980 indicate that he was still working on maintaining Pitt Cottage and its surrounds in order to keep it in good repair.

"Started and Finished Rebuilding and pointing up of back of work-shed wall July 10th to July 31st" Then concreted top of Shed wall, July 25th.

Between August, 16th 1980 and 22nd August, 1980, Tony Drinkwater the local builder who lived at Gawsworth (in the corner at the closed end of our terrace next to Chapel Cottage), reroofed our cottage and was paid £1,260.00 for the job. He did the whole row at the same time including his own cottage and Middle Cottage. (It was not until I had renovations done myself in 2007 to reveal the old ingle nook fire place that we realized that Tony had put a lot of the old tiles down the chimney, instead of carrying them off the roof.). It was an extremely wet day (23rd July, 2007) when my Builder, Graham Stayt and Arthur Bates (a friend who was helping at the time) opened up the fireplace wall and the tiles came tumbling forward.

In 1984, I returned home to live with my parents. I was also studying, day release, for my professional housing qualification at Matthew Boulton College in Birmingham and also a Bachelor of Science Degree with the Open University. I had obtained employment with Warwick District Council that allowed me to return home from Devon.

During the Winter months, if we had snow and in his younger retirement days my Father used to go out and clear the snow from my car, the top of the lane and spread salt so that I could get my car out to go to work in Leamington Spa. (Warwick District Council, in Leamington Spa, 23 miles away from Blockley) and to ensure our neighbours had a safe footing.

In those days, Charlie Dee, a local farmer, who lived at Park Farm, came along with his tractor and a snow plough and cleared the street. Now, in 2022 nothing like that happens and our street can be impassible by ordinary cars for days.

My Father's diaries at this time are full of the activities he is undertaking, whether it is further renovations to the cottage and its surroundings, (at this time he had secondary glazing made and fitted to the downstairs windows and the bathroom). He refurbished the old stone wall in the wash-house by cladding it with concrete blocks and the old garage was maintained and a board front constructed, instead of the old canvas curtain, where he now had his workshop. My Father was a competent electrician so anything that had to be wired in he did and his old friend Maurice Davies would come and check it over and certify the work.

When he was not working in his shed, my Father and Mother could be found in the garden between Archway Cottage and Spindlebrook. They kept a very productive vegetable garden and the kitchen was never without potatoes, carrots, parsnips, runner beans and cabbage as well as some soft fruit like blackcurrants, gooseberries and rhubarb.

They had also kindly agreed to take care of the two dogs, Sally a terrier and Smoky (kennel name: Eskandar Blue Flame) a working Cocker spaniel and my cat Katie when I came home. As I was at work in Leamington Spa all day, my Mother took the dogs for a walk twice a day and sometimes my Father accompanied her. When he accompanied her they went on longer walks through the Dovedale and Bourton Wood. I still have (2023) a string of horse-chestnuts ('known as 'conkers') that they collected on the last walk my Mother and Father took up to the Warren. They had made a seating area for themselves just where the path to the Warren divides to go along to Milton's Barn. The views, there, across the Blockley Valley to Cadley Hill and all the way to Brailes Clump and beyond are lovely).

It was at the beginning of the 1980's that my Father began to suffer problems with his health, beginning with prostrate and he also had a heart attack in the mid 1980's. He recovered well from the heart attack, (although I remember 'preparing myself and my Mother 'for the worst' driving home from Cheltenham Hospital).

When he returned home after a few days he was more careful with his diet in the future and continued to carry on his life much as he had before. In 1986, I took them on holiday to Scotland, we stayed with my, by then, ex-in laws, Des and Phyllis Fell, who, at that time, lived at Garbity Fishing Lodge on the Spey. They had been on holiday to Scotland once before to East Lodge at the Dupplin Estate near Perth where Des (a Forester) and Phyllis lived then.

My Mother at the age of 77 became ill in 1989. She woke up one morning and had had a stroke in the night and did not know what had happened to her. The Doctor found she had congestive heart failure and cardiomyopathy. She spent many weeks at home being cared for by my Father and she had difficulty in swallowing. Then the Doctor (Dr. Barling from Mann Cottage Surgery in Moreton-in-Marsh) decided that she should be admitted to hospital and she spent several weeks in the John Radcliffe hospital. I visited every evening but cannot say I was happy with her care as the ward floor was dirty and she was cold as the bedclothes had not been pulled over her. I spoke to the Doctors there several times but they had decided there was nothing that could be done. My Father was also not well at this time as he had severe sciatica in his 'gammy' leg, so it was decided that my Mother should be discharged to Moreton-in-Marsh Cottage Hospital (this was the old hospital along Hospital Road, also called West Street in Moreton-in-Marsh. I collected her from the John Radcliffe in Oxford and sadly had to tell her that she would not be returning to her home at Blockey, as she thought, but that she was to be admitted to Moreton-in-Marsh Hospital. I know this distressed her (and me) but there was, at the time, no alternative.

I would like to say that she had the best care while she was at Moreton Hospital but this was not the case and I think she was neglected in that when she died she was severely dehydrated. I did visit her at Moreton-in-Marsh, on my way home from my work in Leamington Spa, every evening. My Father did not visit as, as he said, 'it would break him up'. He did get to see my Mother the night before she died but she had fallen into a coma and was unresponsive.

I am absolutely certain that my Father had not expected his beloved wife, Dora, to die before him as he had forfeited part of his pension with the Ministry for her provision after his death. (By then I think the Ministry of Public Building and Works, was integrated into the then Department for the Environment) We did try to claim this back but unfortunately it was done before 1978 and they advised that it could not be returned.

My Mother had a church service at Blockley Church where she had been married to my Father, Ernest Hicks. on the 31st May, 1947 and was cremated at Oakley Wood Crematorium owned by Warwick District Council. (My staff, I was responsible for the sheltered and very sheltered housing and community alarm system at Warwick kindly came to the funeral to support me and my Father).

My Father then looked after me for the next 17 years. He cooked and cleaned the house, walked the dogs and looked after the cat until they themselves died of old age. He made cushions and mended anything that was broken, made candlesticks from chair legs and picture frames and looked after motor cars I had and generally, with infinite kindness supported me in everything I did.

My Father must have felt my mother's death deeply but he never displayed his emotions. When we went to Moreton Hospital on the morning she had died he sadly said: 'we have had over 47 happy years together'. In all my life, I never saw him either angry or overly happy and never 'out of control of his emotions'. I am sure that this stoicism dated back to his very early days spent in hospital without being able to see his Mother for six weeks and also the months spent in the Wingfield Hospital after his major operation in 1948, and his disability.

My Father and myself had two holidays together, after my Mother had died, one to Wales and one to East Anglia. I had thought to take a sabbatical from my job of six months to a year but after discussing this with my Father he was unhappy about my doing this as he felt it would affect my career and so the decision 'not to' was taken for me.

The holiday we had in East Anglia involved a visit to a glass works (Langham Glass) and this so fascinated my Father (and me) that we visited 3 times to see the glass being blown.

My Father had a fall in 2006 and was found and helped up, by our old village Postman, Glen Thomson. My Father recovered from the fall but became ill and needed hospitalisation in October, 2006. A diagnosis was not established. He spent a considerable time in Moreton-in-Marsh hospital. It was also very cold in the hospital and he was cold. They wanted to hoist him into the bath and he was very fearful that the hoist may drop him, but on the first occasion I accompanied him and he was hoisted into the bath without mishap. But, as I have said above, the bathroom and the ward was freezing cold. I had to purchase two dressing gowns for him to wear over his pyjamas.

It was decided to transfer him to Cheltenham Hospital for further investigations. My Employers, Warwick District Council were extremely supportive at this time and allowed me to work what hours I could and gave me time off. As a result I was able to spend most nights at the hospital helping my Father where possible. This went on all over the Christmas period of 2006 and my ex Husband who also lived in the area also visited during the day to assist where possible.

However, I cannot say that my Father got the best of care. Shortly before his death he was put on to a mattress that was supposed to be filled with air but the nurses forgot to pump up the mattress, as a result he spent a whole night with his frail body resting on the bars that were inside the uninflated air mattress. I did complain to the Ward Sister but she told me that she had her best staff on that night and asked me not to complain. After a consultation with my Father he too did not want to complain for fear it would make things worse for him.

A few days later he died after he was transferred to another ward. I believe the staff on that ward did what they could to make him comfortable before his death. I had returned home for a short spell of two hours and he died while I was away. My ex husband, Keith Fell, was, however, at his bedside and I am grateful for that. He said, my Father said to him, ' Has Ginny gone, (my pet name was Ginny). Keith said 'Yes, she has gone'. He then said 'Then I can go too then' and died. He was 94 years old.

Since 2007 I have lived alone in the cottage that my Grandparents bought in 1928 and which has been the family home since then. I have chosen to end my Father's Story with this Epilogue rather than detail his 30 years of retirement. He lived through two World Wars and the hard times endured by his parents. He never let his disability hold him back and through circumstance was forced to carry out heavy manual work but also work that he found rewarding at the Pump House and at the Fire College that required attention to detail and skill.

He learnt personal discipline and consequent stoicism at an early age, some of which I am sure was inherited from my Grandmother. He was an exceptional man who married my Mother, Doris Anne Moore. who had also known adversity and I am proud that he was my Father and she my Mother.

PART 11

MY MOTHER'S STORY – DORIS (ALWAYS KNOWN AS 'DORA' ANNIE HICKS nee MOORE)

Doris (always called 'Dora') taken for Ruby Wedding 31st May, 1987

Extract from documents provided by the Children's Society on 18th August, 2017.

"The application form to the Children's Society was filled out on my Mother's behalf on 25th January, 1916. (My Mother had been born on the 13th March, 1913 and so was almost 3 years of age when the application was made).

'The application form confirms that your mother was born on 13th March 1913 at Cookley Farm, High Wood, Eastham and was baptized at Hanley Child Church, Tenbury on 6th April, 1913.

There are no siblings listed on Doris's application form.

Doris was illegitimate. (As you are aware this was the term used at this time and so it will appear in the summary although it is no longer current). Her mother was Caroline Anne Moore aged 31. Caroline was a general servant living with her employer, Mrs. Hall, Ashton, Leominster. She earned £12.00 per year. Doris's father was stated to be Andrew Lloyd, aged about 34. He had been working as a farm labourer, but had 'gone away' 'cannot be found'. At the time of application Doris was living with Mrs (illegible), Lime Tree Cottage, High Wood, Eastham, Tenbury.

The application form lists Doris's other relatives as: Maternal Aunt, Mrs. Owens, Castle Bromwich age 29, Cowman's wife. (Caroline's Sister).

Members of Doris's wider family were not in a position to contribute towards her maintenance should she be accepted by The Waifs and Strays Society as the Children's Society was formally known. Her mother could give £5.00 a year for four years. If Doris was discharged from a Home for any reason there would be no-one able to receive her. She would 'become chargeable to the parish of Tenbury, Worcs' – in other words she would be the responsibility of the local poor law authorities.

Doris was referred to the Society by Mrs. Sarah S. Hughes, Penlee, Tenbury. She wrote the following report on Doris's circumstances. 'The infant is the illegitimate child of Caroline Moore, the daughter of an agricultural workman (now deceased) who was in receipt of the old age pension whom she kept house for and helped to support by working in the fields. The father of the child instead of keeping his promise to marry Caroline has gone away and cannot be found'. The child is at present in the care of a man aged 75 receiving the old age pension, and his wife about 60 who receives 2 shillings and 6 pence per week for looking after the child.

The application form was signed by Caroline Moore committing Doris wholly to the care of the Society and her signature was witnessed by Sarah Hughes. Caroline also consented to Dora being emigrated to Canada if found suitable. Doris was medically examined as part of the application process and her general health was stated to be good. *(My Mother told me that the Matron of the Home at Dinas Orphanage, Brecon, prevented her being emigrated to Canada as 'she loved her so much').*

The Case Committee of The Waifs and Strays Committee agreed to accept Doris provided 4 shillings per week was paid towards her maintenance.

Sarah Hughes had initially made enquiries of a Mr. Hunt on 25th December, 1915 by asking if Doris could be admitted to a particular Home (not named, as Sarah Hughes appeared to know a child already in this Home). She, Sarah Hughes, stated that Caroline Moore was 'quite without means and has been keeping house for father who only has had the old age pension and the last few weeks he lived in Tenbury Union (Workhouse) as he was so crippled with rheumatism, so reduced her to furniture her father had, which is very poor stuff and no money. I found her a situation and her some clothes from two ladies who are interested in this class of girl, and the baby some people have for 2/6 per week and they are housing the bit of furniture. The father of the child, was not made to pay to it at the time and now is not to be found'. She wrote again on 9th January, 1916 having received a reply which is not in the file. 'The father of the girl is dead and buried at Hanly (Hanley) Child on Dec 9th 1915, so it leaves the daughter and child. *(I believe after some research that this was a fabrication because a Death Certificate for that date cannot be found for Andrew Lloyd. A Death Certificate for this name is available in 1921 registered at Bromyard and I think this is when he actually died, if so it was while he was working on a Farm and he had a heart condition. If so, I believe, Sarah Hughes, or Caroline, herself fabricated the death information to get Doris accepted by the Waifs and Strays Society, probably as the best and only option for the child. I also believe, again from research using Ancestry, that Andrew Lloyd was in Hospital in Tenbury Wells on the Census Date in 19ll and at that time his age is listed as 36. His age at death is listed as 46).* Sarah goes on to say, 'The girl (Caroline) is quite a success at the situation and will have been there a month on Tuesday 11th January, but her wages are only £12. a year to start so she could not possibly pay 4/- a week to mind the child, but I don't think it is a right place for a little one 3½ years old. I must still look out for a place for the child. Do you know of anywhere?'

A further letter was written on 25th January, presumably to accompany the completed application form. 'Caroline Moore has just been a month at her situation during that time she has given satisfaction to Mrs. Hall her mistress. She came to see me today and we had a long talk. She is prepared to offer £5 a year paid by monthly instalments for 4 years, and as you will see this will bring her very low in purse, but I know one or two ladies who will help me to clothe her and in this way it will not relieve her of her burden so easily. She is not a callous girl by any means and does feel her position. (In those days welfare agencies were careful not to appear to be excusing 'sin'! (However, Revd. Edward Rudolf the Founder and Secretary of the Society, was not of this view and was happy to accept many illegitimate children into the care of the Society). The letter goes on to say. 'I notice what you say in your letter about her wages being small, but she has not before done housework, it has been 'charring' (cleaning) of a rough kind and outdoor work to help the cottage home along, and take care of the old father, but I hope to get an advance for her in 12 months time. You will notice that Caroline has consented to the child going abroad if thought desirable. (Consent to emigration was stated to hasten acceptance of a child.). (*At least through the love and benefaction of the Matron of the first home at Dinas my Mother escaped that*).

The Case Committee of the Waifs and Strays Committee agreed to accept Doris provided 4 shillings a week was paid towards her maintenance 'in accordance with your usual terms in regard to children of illegitimate birth'. Sarah Hughes agreed to arrange this and to obtain guarantees for the 4/- a week payment for 4 years.

On 3 May, 1916 Sarah Hughes informed Edward Rudolf that the local Board of Guardians (administrators of the Poor Law) had agreed to contribute 1/6 a week to maintain Doris in a Waifs and Strays Society Home. Caroline would pay the remaining 2/6 a week. A few weeks later the Guardians decided to contribute 2/6 a week. Doris had some medical issues ('slight eczema about the groins' and 'incontinence of urine') that the doctor pointed out were in consequence of neglect by the person she was living with. As the woman was unsuitable, Sarah Hughes needed to remove Doris to another cottage home until she entered one of the Society's Homes, and she was therefore, anxious that the little girl should be found a permanent Home as soon as possible. *(It was not unusual for the Poor Law authorities to contribute towards the maintenance of children in the care of The Waifs and Strays Society. It was felt better that they be brought up away from the stigma of the workhouse. Such children were placed in Certified Homes).*

On 31st May, 1916 Doris was admitted to the Dinas Orphanage, Brecon, They were very pleased to take her 'she is just what our Matron longs for and we gratefully accept her'. All the children were excited to meet 'our baby'. Oh, we shall love her'. *(I firmly believe it was this matron that prevented my Mother from being sent to Canada).* On 30th August, 1917 Sarah Hughes wrote to Edward Rudolf to ask if Doris could be transferred to the Harrow Home (*London*) where another Tenbury child was living as 'it would be easier to find people able to visit her in a Home near London. 'Her Mother is doing very well keeping her situation and not any desire to go back or see any of her old friends'. There were no vacancies available at the Harrow Home at this time. In 1918 the Executive Committee of the Society reluctantly decided to close the Dinas Home and on 12th December, 1918 Doris was transferred to Tregarth Home, Bangor.

On 25th January, 1919 Canon Eastwood of the Tregarth Home informed Edward Rudolf that a Mrs. Williams who had visited the Home had asked if it might be possible to adopt Doris. (Adoption had no legal force before 1926 and adoptions were arranged privately. *(I think it is at this time that my Mother was given a china doll for Christmas, but sadly, she remembered vividly that another child had stepped on it and broken it). My Mother told me that she remembered the kind lady who gave it to her and she had hoped she would be adopted at the time but this, sadly, did not happen).* Doris's Mother was still alive so nothing could be arranged without her permission but Mrs. Williams remained very anxious to adopt Doris and was able to offer her a very comfortable home. Enquiries were made through Sarah Hughes to find out what Caroline Moore's feeling were on the matter.

Sarah Hughes met Caroline on 7th March, 1919. She reported that Caroline was not against the adoption but wanted the answer to some questions. 'Was Mrs. Williams a widow and how many children did she have of her own. If she was not a widow what did her husband do? Caroline had apparently been 'very troublesome of late, changing her places'. She was at that time living in a Vicarage six miles from Tenbury. Sarah Hughes intended 'sticking to (Caroline) for the little girls' sake' but she thought it would be a good thing if Doris was adopted. Mrs. Williams was not a widow, her husband was a 'retired provision dealer, now keeping a farm, and they had no family'. On 13th April, Sarah Hughes informed Edward Rudolf that Caroline would not agree to the adoption and would not give a reason for her decision. Sarah Hughes found Caroline difficult to talk to and said she was just trying to keep her in her situation because of the maintenance money Caroline had to contribute towards Doris's care. In August, 1919 Caroline changed her mind and consented to the adoption. Edward Rudolf informed the Tregarth Home, but he stated that he felt it might be unwise to proceed as Caroline could change her mind again which might cause a lot of unhappiness. The authorities at the Home agreed and there was an added difficulty that Mrs. Williams was a 'Calvinstic Methodist' and did not attend an Anglican Church. Sarah Hughes was unhappy with this decision. She was finding it hard to obtain the maintenance money from Caroline who was constantly changing her employment, however, once the situation was fully explained to her she accepted it.

In mid 1920, the period of 4 years for which Caroline had agreed to pay towards Doris's maintenance came to an end. The Tenbury Board of Guardians agreed to increase the amount they contributed to 10 shillings a week and undertook to collect whatever they could from Caroline.

On 24th August, 1921 Doris was transferred to. St. Christopher's Home, Altringham as it was decided to close the Tregarth Home. The Tenbury Guardians had received regular reports on Doris. In 1927 they informed the Matron of St. Christopher's that they would be glad if Doris could be found a situation as soon as possible as she had reached school leaving age. (The Society did not consider this possible as Doris was not 15 until the following March and was not trained sufficiently to take a situation of any kind).

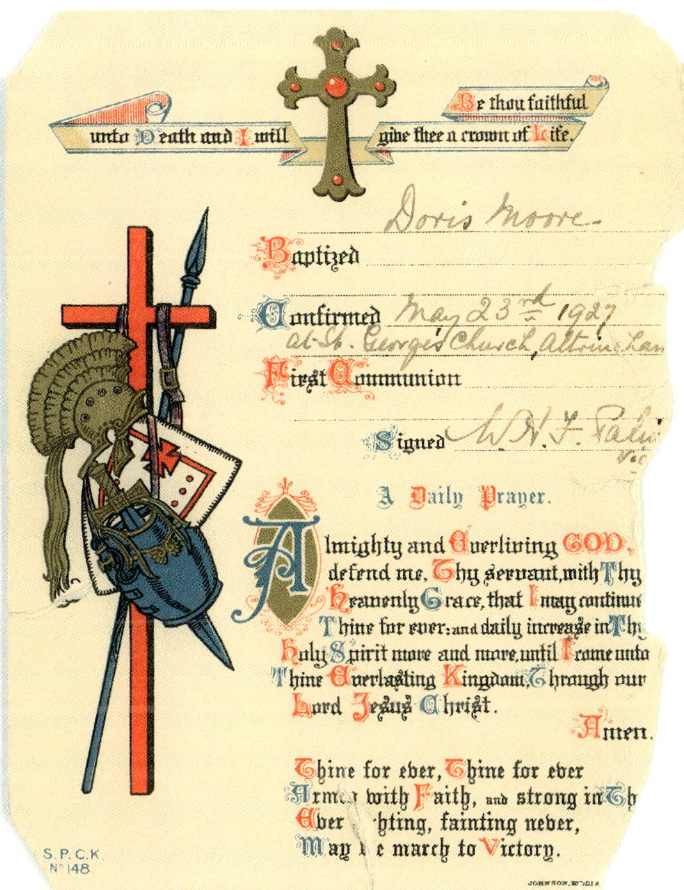

My Mothers Confirmation Certificate: St. George's Church, Altringham, 23rd May, 1927

(The Society's girls were not placed out in situations before the age of 16. It was considered important that they have two years training in the Home after leaving school).

In November, 1928 the Guardians informed the Society that they would discontinue payments for Doris from the date of her sixteenth birthday. (It is interesting that until this date the Guardians had received positive reports about Doris's progress but after that date the Hon. Secretary of St. Christopher's Home informed the Secretary of the Society that Doris could not be recommended for domestic service as she 'was simple minded and will always require supervision'). The Home Committee recommended that the Tenbury Guardians be asked to take her back.

(The Guardians then sought clarification as this contradicted the previous reports they had received from the Matron). Copies of two reports were sent that the Guardians had received from Janet Bullock, the Matron of St. Christopher's. On 4th March, 1926 Doris was 'doing very well at school, but not brilliant, has made great progress the last year and much improved in every way'. She was 'sensitive, kind and unselfish; and her intelligence was described as 'fair'. She was said to be suitable for 'domestic service or laundry work'.

(My Mother told me that at this time she was friendly with another girl but this girl either disappeared or (perhaps she died). This upset my Mother a lot as she told me. She was told by the Matron of the Home that 'the girl had 'gone to the dogs' meaning that something had gone badly wrong and lost all the good things it had).

In March, 1927 Doris reached the age of 14. The Hon Secretary of the Home asked if she might be placed in a Laundry Home and the information was passed to the Tenbury Guardians. Doris was admitted to St. Edith's Home in Fareham on 8th January, 1929. It was originally intended that she was to move in December but the Matron of St. Christopher's asked for her to remain so she could enjoy all the Christmas Treats and parties with the girls she knew. The Sunday School party and prize giving was on 20th December and 'it would be nice for her to receive her own prize having earned it. Doris is a very sensitive child. I am sure she would feel it very much and be very unhappy, if she left us before Christmas.'

(My Mother told me about pushing heavy laundry baskets up and down streets in Fareham and also collecting bread for the home from the Bakery. I do not think she was unhappy there. It was from a book she had there that I obtained the name of the Children's Society Home and was able to find out this information).

On 20th August, 1930 Doris was discharged to a situation in service with a Mrs. Harris, 30 Crescent Way, Norbury, South London She was to work as a Geneal Maid. There is some correspondence *(that I have not seen)* from July, to October, 1932 concerning Doris's employment. She was a member of the local Girls Friendly Society and they spoke very highly of her considering her a most worthy and exemplary member. It appears that there was an impression in some quarters that Doris's employers expected her to do too much work and did not always treat her in a consistent manner. Doris gave notice and the Society's travelling Matron visited her. The Society was prepared to find her a new situation, they were anxious for her to leave. Mrs. Harris did not want Doris to leave and wrote to the Society. Doris withdrew her notice. Doris was said to be 'very tender hearted and presumably was pressured by her employers'. The Society was anxious that she should consider her own welfare and asked her to come and visit the Welfare Secretary to discuss matters. In a letter to Miss Nunns of the Girls Friendly Society, the Welfare Secretary wrote 'there are plenty of other good situations waiting for her and I want to try and impress upon her that she must try and think of herself and try to do a little better than she is doing now, so I will let you know when I see her, and should you by any chance come across her, would you try and persuade her to come up and see me as soon as she can'. Miss Nunns replied saying that she felt that Doris needed 'calm' and it is only for that reason that we should wish your kind help to be deferred until a little later.

(I think at some point that Doris must have left Mrs. Harris as that is not the name of the family she is with at the outbreak of WW2. I think Mrs. Harris may have been the Doctor's wife who nearly 'brained' her with a bottle of alcohol.).

The file the Children's Society hold also contain a summary of reports about Doris written between 1916 and 1930. Doris was considered to be 'a nice child'. Her disposition was described using the following adjectives, 'good tempered, affectionate, sensitive, nervous, quiet, kind, unselfish, truthful, honest and obedient. Her health and conduct were good or very good. She was considered perfectly able to go out to work 'in service' following her training at St. Ediths.

Note: St. Christopher's Home, Altringham

(As her daughter I would completely confirm this summing up. My Mother never lost her temper, was so kind that she would 'give you the clothes off her back' and I never heard her say a bad word against anyone. I miss her greatly. She was a truly exceptional woman. I once asked my Mother if she would like to find her Mother but she said 'if she had wanted me she would have kept me'. I believe that her Mother, Caroline Moore, went on to marry a George Birch at Kidderminster in 1920. She had another child by Mr. Birch in 1925 called Elizabeth. Caroline, died in 1939 aged 55. Her last address on the 1939 'scratch' Register, was 195 Wood Lane, Hurcott, Kidderminster, Worcestershire). Elizabeth Birch married a Mr. Cartwright in 1943 and Elizabeth died in 1997 and the death was registered in Kidderminster.

APPENDIX

BLOCKLEY BUS ACCIDENT 1924

There were specific village events that affected my Father considerably, including the Blockley Bus Crash of Tuesday 5th August, 1924. My Father was 12 at the time the accident occurred. He, of course, knew all of those killed in this accident.

The driver of the bus was Dennis Sharp (Shaver) who after the accident had gone to work at Butler's as a lorry driver. It was 'Shaver' that had got him his first job at Butlers. My Father always said that 'Shaver' was never the same man afterwards. 'Shaver' suffered head injuries in the accident and a metal plate was put into his head, I believe this was done at a London hospital. Unfortunately, this affected his pituitary gland and when he died, at I believe the age of 47, he was over 7 ft. in height. He is buried in the Station Road, Cemetery at Blockley.

To the day he died my Father regretted that there was no memorial to the victims. In 2022 the Vicar of the Parish, Dana Delap arranged for a plaque to be installed on the wall where the bus overturned commemorating the accident. However, the grave containing most of the victims, apart from Mrs. Figgures who was buried with her husband at the Cemetery in Station Road, and the woman who was visiting from Birmingham (buried in Birmingham on the same day as the funeral of the victims at Blockley) is in

Wreaths on the grave of the Blockley Bus Crash victims buried in the Blockley, Station Road, Cemetery

the left hand top corner (by the dividing wall) of the old part of the Cemetery in Station Road and remains unmarked.

Those killed outright were: Mrs. George Launcelot Figgures (66), nee Mary Jane Haines, known as 'Aunt Polly'; Mrs. Frank Hopes (30) and her son Bernard Leslie Hopes (3); Mrs. W. Smith (36) and her son Harry Smith (5); Miss Evelyn Lavinia Green from Birmingham who was staying with the Taylor family in Park Road and Miss Doris Hancock (16) who died during the night.

BLOCKLEY FIRES

There were two major fires in the village when my Father was a boy and a barn fire at Pasture Farm. The first he mentions was a Canadian style bungalow built by Roland Dyer when he came back from Canada after WW1. This fire occurred on 6th March, 1926.

One school lunchtime whilst Mother, Brother John and me were having lunch about 1.00 p.m. it came about that about 100 yards from where we lived in High Street, a newly built Canadian style place (or house) had been built to form part living quarters and fruit and vegetable shop. Now being only built with a wooden strutted frame – together with weather proof materials on outside. It had suddenly caught fire. The whole structure was nearly one mass of fire in a few minutes. The cause of the fire I understand was caused by fish pan catching fire as the girl shop assistant prepared her lunch. Mother, me and brother got up from lunch table and went to the door to investigate the blaze which was going well.

Now Mother said 'you boys get off back to school', because by now the old Blockley Hand Manual Fire Engine came by being pushed and hurried along by some local firemen and helpers to the big blaze and Fire Water point in Turvey's Hill. (The hydrant is still there 2023). Now this is the point where Mother said again 'back to school you boys'. Of course, Brother John obeyed Mother's commands but I am sorry to say that I did not oblige to the Mother's command and return to school. I had things on my mind and decided I was going to go to that blazing inferno. So, out of sight of Mother that disobedient boy (me) went along the street up through the Crown Inn (Hotel) yard and out into the back ends road, climbed over into the adjoining field ran along the field to the back end of the site of the Fire, jumped from the wall onto the bank footpath, then down onto this to where the Manual Fire Engine was stationed and where several of my mates were helping to pump the water from engine to the fire. So being a strong boy I helped pump from the old Blockley water main hydrant until the Dovedale Reservoir ran dry. Therefore, buckets of water from Russell Spring was poured into the hopper of the engine to pump. But by now the fire was so big that the Fire Chief called upon the services of the Moreton-in-Marsh Engine to come and assist. The engine had to be towed all the way from Moreton via Bourton on the Hill into Blockley. Therefore by the time it arrived the building was over half burnt down. Now when the Moreton Fire Engine arrived for it to pump water it was found none available left in Blockley main pipe. So, the Fire Chief of Moreton got his men to pull up the wooden fence from the road front of Mr. George Sharps garden (this is now my garden) and then pushed the engine all the way down the length of the garden, and started to pump from the mill stream. The boys all helped to pump from there to try and save some of the place if possible. In fact, in the end, nothing was saved. The fire was so dense with heat that some of the houses doors and windows over the road were cracked and the door paint melted, also the house of old Mr. Beachy next door his house wall was so hot inside the bedrooms that the firemen were sent to watch in case a fire started in that house. The stones on the outer wall burnt.

Now again on returning to school the next morning, we boys found out that the Head Teacher had been informed by the two under teachers concerning us 20/30 boys whom did not answer to the register roll call the afternoon before. When the teacher had received this information he came out of his room stood in front of the other classes of us boys. Now he starts. He calls out each boys name that did not answer to the register yesterday afternoon and says 'please present yourself out in front of me'. By the time he had finished calling out all the names, it happened the line of us boys was nearly as long as the room we were in. He put down the registers and asked why so many of us had been truant from school and on being told the situation 'why we were away' he said 'that was men's jobs and not us boy's.

Now, again we boys thought this is where the cruel bit is about to be rendered by him, because he said 'my intentions are to give you all the cane on each hand and make you all stay after school each day and write a composition concerning your behaviour and as to why you were doing men's work instead of attending school'. Therefore after he had completed said task he left the room, leaving his other two teachers to deal with us boys after school. Therefore we lot thought the school master had rendered punishment on them as well as us, because they had to stay with us the next two/three nights.

(The site that this Canadian type house was built on was a good mixed fruit orchard owned by an old gentleman by the name of Mr. Hardy of Arlington House. Mr. Hardy used to sell the orchard of fruit every year. When he became old he decided to sell up and that is when it was bought by Mr. Rowland Dyer over at Draycott and the Canadian type house was built and later burnt down and this site all boarded up and left for years until part of site was cleared and a shoe and boot cobblers shop built there by Mr. Ledbetter. (Who had made my first boot and who lived at Mount Pleasant.)

ANOTHER FIRE: DOVEDALE HOUSE

One morning just after (5 a.m.) I was woken by the sound of the big fire bell sounding as I lay in bed up in the attic of the house at the top of Mill Lane (Cheshers Lane). On jumping out of bed, dressing and went out into the street to investigate where the fire may be only to find the fire crew with the single handed fire engine come running by full hell for leather on their way to the big Dovedale House at the far end of the village. So, therefore thinking about nothing else I ran and joined them helping to push the engine all up the street until we reached the fire. My word it was a big fire which was in the best part of the highly polished section. The engine was all set up at the side of the big pond of water, Now, shouts the Fire Chie,f all hands to the pump, and of course being not many people about it meant us strong boys whom had also come with us other lot and engine having to partake. After about twenty minutes to half hour it was noticed that the small amount of water that the single handed pump was throwing was not doing much good to quell the big inferno of fire only helping to stop the fire from spreading to the main hall and servants quarters. Therefore, the Fire Chief phoned for assistance from Moreton-in-Marsh brigade but by the time it took them to appear from Moreton and set up their appliance it was found that the best part of the house, and together with the roof had already fallen in. So, the two Fire chiefs had a talk together and they decided to let that part of the house quietly burn out and let them concentrate playing their hoses of saving the other part of the house, until the Fire Chiefs thought it safe to stop the pump and then hourly inspect the whole lot of damage the fire had caused, to the best part of house. Then the two Fire Chiefs called all us boys together in the presence of the owner Mr. Deaking. Mr. Deaking said he would make arrangements for our local Fire Chief to recompense us later in the week. But I am sorry to say as the days and months went by us boys involved never received a thing for all our kindness rendered at the fire.

But we boys did receive a big unexpected something in the afternoon when we reported back to school, us boys about 20/25 of us strong top end of village rough necks were all called out of our classes and made to line up all down the room and told by the Head Master whom had been informed of our truancy of the mornings behaviour. He started off by giving us a lecture about it, that our place was to attend school and not to do things that did not concern us. Then he said his intentions were to administer the cane upon our hands and also all of you will forfeit all other playtimes and sports sessions and I will expect an essay from you of your actions so that they can be sent to the Church of England Authority to see if any further actions will be taken against all of you boy's misbehaviour. Well now after we were kept in suspense for several months a letter did arrive at the school one morning and the Master had us line up and stood in front of us rough necks and read the letter out loud. It stated that the authority's thought no further action should be taken against all us boys whom had rendered a kindness to the people concerned. I must say that made the school bosses face drop, turn on his heel and left the whole of us line of boys standing out still in the front of the other boys in class, until one of the under teachers took control and told us to return to our desks. (Another escapade completed by us roughnecks and awaiting the next to come forth (amen).

PASTURE FARM

1925 This is another episode of truancy from school which happened by us fire fighting mad boys again in 1925.

Now, it came about again one Monday morning in the year 1925 early between the hours of 6.30 a.m. and 7 o'clock just as myself and the other family present were having our breakgast we all suddenly heard the fire Bell on the Old Bake House wall sound. Therefore without hesitation this same young chap jumps up from the table and bolts along to the fire station to find some of the fire crew preparing the old engine ready to go to attend a big barn fire (full of hay) up the fields. Pasture Farm was farmed by Mr. Minett. Now again without further thought and as of previous fires this chap was gone again together with my pals who had arrived as well, to help in some way, or other with the engine and also at the fire. I'm afraid this young truant player thought that school was only secondary for a while, and so did my trusty friends. (The Hales and the Gills).

Well, all the hands that were available at the time put all their hands to the engine and ran with it to Pasture Lane on Lower Street pushed and shoved it all the way up Pasture Lane all the way up the Pasture Farm road until we arrived at the barn fires. The Fire Chief after he inspected the situation and inquired of a water supply to pump from, to his horror he was told by Mr. Minett that no surplus water of quantity was available to pump. Mr. Minett said the only supply of water that was being used at the farm came from a well away up in another field and supplied the kitchen and dairy for milk cooling etc. So after more talk between the fire crew and us helpers the Fire Chief said 'let's try buckets and milk churns to get water to the engine from the kitchen tap supply, now well that was undertaken, but to no avail after about 15/20 minutes. So that Fire Chief and his firemen decided to quietly let the fire burn out whilst still under strong guard until all the fire crew thought it was safe to leave in Mr. Minett and his workmens charge. Therefore the engine also its fire crew and together with us boys and other helpers whom had come to help later, all returned back down (hanging on to the engine this time) to Blockley at around 12.00 p.m. Now when I appeared for lunch I received a very severe telling off from Mother and also Mother threatened to tell Father of my escapade when he returned home that night from his work. (That left me shaking in my boots). I am very pleased to say my kind Mother never told on me. Now this is where the same procedure again started by the Head Teacher as started as in 1924 Dovedale House truancy of us boys. When we returned to school in the afternoon. He started off with a lecture, lined us all up again rendered his punishment accordingly. After he had administered his punishment upon all of us boys. He done an unusual thing, he sat down on the corner of one desk and asked us all just one question (what makes you boys do such things as to why you must do mens jobs). The answer to his question came from one of our oldest gang of boys, of whom was just about to leave school and his name was Norman Hitchman who lived by Russell Spring. He said to the teacher as he represented us other boys. Mr. Wyatt Sir, should the fires we have given our help to have been at your house, or property, would you still have tendered your punishment like you have to us boys for helping to save perhaps lives or property. Well, when he had thought for a while his answer was very poor we thought. He only said he would still expect us boys to attend school, and therefore leave those jobs for the proper people to deal with. With that sort of answer he turned round and left and returned to his class room.

EXTRA ANECDOTES

NO TEA

My Father recalled that when they moved into Pitt Cottage in the 1920's the fireplace in the living room was an Inglenook and a pot used to hang on a chain over the fire. My Grandmother had a pot of Sheeps head stew on one day (including my Father said the eyeballs). It was a Sunday and unfortunately the chimney caught fire and soot came down into the Stew (a disaster!). Father recalled that they had to have bread and jam for tea that night!

My Grandfather altered the fireplace considerably in 1948 when he had the fireplace closed and a 'Carrona' Enamelled Range with Boiler, surround kerb and tiles installed. See copy of Invoice from Stanley F. Wass, General Ironmonger of Moreton-in-Marsh, below.

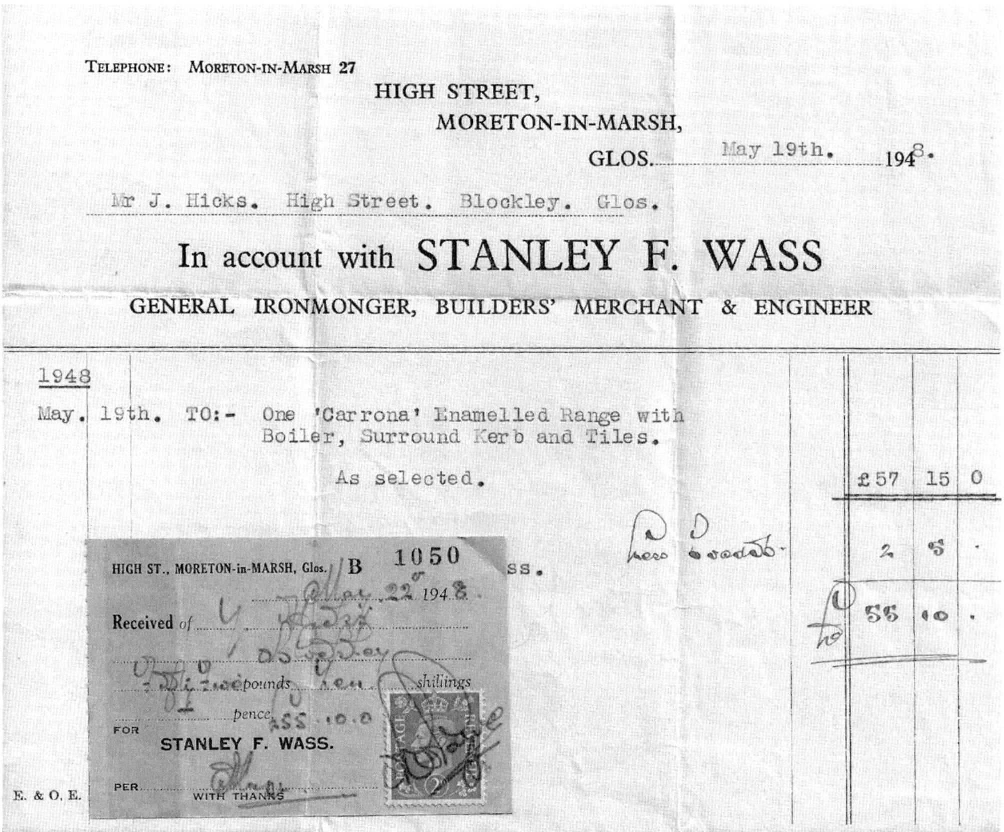

TELEPHONE: MORETON-IN-MARSH 27

HIGH STREET,
MORETON-IN-MARSH,
GLOS. May 19th. 1948.

Mr J. Hicks. High Street. Blockley. Glos.

In account with STANLEY F. WASS

GENERAL IRONMONGER, BUILDERS' MERCHANT & ENGINEER

1948			£	s	d
May.	19th.	TO:- One 'Carrona' Enamelled Range with Boiler, Surround Kerb and Tiles. As selected.	£57	15	0
			2	5	.
			55	10	.

HIGH ST., MORETON-in-MARSH, Glos. B 1050

May 22 1948

Received of

pounds shillings

pence £55.10.0

FOR STANLEY F. WASS.

PER

WITH THANKS

E. & O. E.

BATTERSEA POWER STATION

During the 1930's Captain Churchill always liked to show the men working at the Brickworks the results of their labours. My Father recalled that they went on at least two trips.

Rouses Coaches were hired to take the men to see the newly constructed Battersea Power Station. Two coaches were needed. Unfortunately, he and his fellow workers on that coach never got to see Battersea Power Station because he was in the second coach and in his words 'it conked for petrol at Marble Arch'.

Instead, one of his mates, I think a Hale, said he had relatives at Upper Norwood and also knew which bus to take to get them there. My Father said they arrived at a flat there. The lady was evidently drying her washing and on their arrival scurried around trying to take it down. Anyway, apparently her husband was there and went out and got sausages and they had a good lunch and then they went to a football match in the afternoon and got back to the coach at Marble Arch at the time that had been prescribed by the driver.

He had evidently found somewhere to fill up with petrol in the meantime to bring them home.

They also had a trip to see the Bristol Arches but that went uneventfully.

THE FAST 12.00

Captain Churchill used to come down from London on a train my Father called the 'fast 12'. It got into Moreton-in-Marsh at 12.00 and came through what was then Blockley Station about 20 minutes later. Captain Churchill's Chauffeur used to pick him up at Moreton-in-Marsh in the car and my Father said you could time it, as the 'Fast 12' came through Blockley Station, Churchill's car came through the gate of the Brickworks. Churchill used to go straight into the Office to see Jack Hull, the Manager of Northwick Brick and Tile Works and then go and walk around the brickworks talking to the men.

THE HEALTH AND SAFETY INSPECTOR

There had been a couple of serious accidents at the Brickworks and one poor lad got his hand cut out under the brick press. It was common practice for the Health and Safety Inspector to come into the yard and report to the office and by the time they got into the works the guard had been put back on the press and any other machinery that needed one. However, one day a Lady Health and Safety Inspector arrived on the scene. She did not report to the office and came on to the works via a footpath that ran alongside the Clay Pit. Of course, she saw the Brick Press without its guard and my Father observed that she went straight to the office and 'there was hell to play'. The guard never came off the brick press again.

THE PUMP HOUSE AT NORTHWICK PARK

Situated across from the front of the Northwick Mansion. Constructed by Higgs and Hill to serve the then new American Army Hospital. Built of Common Brick with concrete access road leading through the old Northwick Rickyard and across two fields to the site. The Well that the water was pumped from at the back of the Pump House is as described in the main text, the water was then treated, measured and piped up to the Reservoir situated in the field below the wood called Augusta high above the camp, so it ran 'gravity' to the then newly constructed American Army Field Hospital.

Every gallon pumped from the Pump House to the Reservoir my Father recorded in a book. Captain Edward George Spencer Churchill was paid 6d (old pence) per thousand gallons for the water pumped and used by the Hospital and later the camp at Northwick.

TOMMY HOPKINS AND THE WINTER OF 1963

Tommy Hopkins used to cycle to work at the Boiler House from Winterway. When he came on shift my Father told Tommy how bad and deep the snow was in the Park but Tommy was confident he could ride home though the park on his bicycle.

A couple of hours after Tommy had left the boiler house my Father had to go up to the Pump House. He decided to go along the road towards the Mansion and across the front of the Mansion to the Pump House as vehicles had been along this road and it was semi clear. On reaching the sharp corner opposite the entrance to the Farm Dairy and Yards my Father heard someone shouting and it was Tommy who had gone off the road down the bank and into a snow drift at the bottom of this corner with his bike on top of him and could not get back up again. My Father lifted the bike off Tommy and helped him back up as best he could and dusted what snow he could off him. He suggested to Tommy that he go up to the Pump House with him to get 'thawed out' but Tommy did not want to do that. My Father said 'Tommy got on his old bike and pedaled off as best he could down the park road'.

THE CHAISE LOUNGE IN PITT COTTAGE SITTING ROOM

At the time of writing the Chaise Lounge occupies a position under the front sitting room window where it has been since purchased from H. J. Paintin in 1928 when my Grandmother and Grandfather and family moved to Pitt Cottage. My Grandmother paid £2.00 for it and my Father and Grandmother carried it up the lane.

It has only been out of the cottage once in the almost 100 years it has been in our possession and this was in 2013 after I retired from work. It went to the workshops of Tapper's in Birmingham for a badly needed reupholster. Unfotunately, this, of course, removed the 'dunt' put into the sofa by my Father's cat 'Tibbers', as she had always slept on the Chaise Lounge (or Sofa, as we used to call it), and her bed spot was the dip in the sofa that she had made by continually sleeping in the same place after my Father left home.

MISCHIEF STORIES

APPLE SCRUMPING

One Sunday afternoon. when we' rough necks' had not much to do. we went into a local farmers orchard for a few of his apples. We had just got busy shaking the tree and picking up some of the fallen apples into our pockets and jersey fronts, when suddenly one of the other boys happened to look up and had the biggest shock of the day. The village Constable was just climbing over the wall some yards away from us, that done it. Down went the apples and away we ran full speed, we ran the full length of the orchard and hid behind big bunches of shrubs. etc., watching to see where the policeman was going or what he was going to do. We stopped behind the shrubs for quite some time and watched him go back over the wall into the road and away along the village and out of sight and then we went our ways looking for something else to do. Now, what worried us on the Monday morning was if he would put in an appearance up at the school to report us to the Head Teacher but we were glad he did not and therefore that was another episode when we escaped the cane.

GUY FAWKES NIGHT

We were all involved in another bit of mischief one Guy Fawkes November Night. We had managed to scrape together some money and we bought fireworks called (Empire Guns). After we let some off in the street and had frightened some people and set dogs barking, we knew a house where an old man lived on his own. It was decided to pay him a visit. We decided upon whom could run the fastest. One of the smallest boys volunteered so – two of the fireworks were lit and then one boy stuffed them in the key hole of the old man's door, whilst us other rough necks kept watch at a safe distance.

Now a few minutes after the fireworks were lit and put in the key hole, there was a big bang and an almighty noise when the lock was heard spinning across the floor. Now I am afraid to say that our fastest runner was not quite fast enough to get away, because as quick as lightening the man came out and managed to catch him and my word he did belt his backside. He done no more than took the boy to his home and told his Dad what he had just done, where his dad cuffed the boys head and sent him to bed. Now all of us others felt sorry for him in some respect. Also, we were thankful it was not our backsides this time.

WINDOW TAPPING

Now there was another bit of mischief we gang did sometimes on a dark evening. We used to get a long piece of thin string or cottons and attached two heavy buttons or iron washers on one end, then found a suitable house where we thought would do for our manoeuvre close by, or at a window in the rooms where the people lived. We then fastened the end of string or cotton over a nail or stick in the wall just above the window, then run the line across the path or road then we hid ourselves in the dark, and then gently pull the line once , or twice, so that the object tied to the line would knock the windows. After a minute or two we awaited the results. If it was one of our good nights the joke could happen two or maybe three times. One night we picked a good place where we knew that several children and parents lived. We pulled the line and waited, out came one of the children of the household, he had a look around and went back indoors. So, we pulled again and waited again and out came the lady of the household she looked around and muttered something and then went back in and shut the door. Now after a few minutes we decided to pull the line again, so we did. My word, this time out came the man of the household all of a hustle and bustle with his arms and hand containing a stick and also shouting abuse or swearing out into the surrounding darkness. All of a sudden he found what the object was that had caused their disturbance and he made it his business to find out where the line came from. He started to follow the line across the space between his place and where we had just bolted from to another safe place to hide and watch his antics. As soon as he got to the end of the line my word he did he shout his abuse and swear, he then eventally went back into the house (we retired for the night) and made our ways to our houses). Another episode of mischief done.

CLOVER PICKING

I well remember one year about a week or two before some summer holidays a local farmer came to the school to ask the head teacher if he would ask his boys if any of them would volunteer to go up to his farm and work for him during the holidays and help pick the heads off the pink clover plants so that he could have it for seed to plant again. As, it happened the Farmer also went to the Girls School and put the same question to that head teacher.

When the day came that was planned for us to go, it happened that there was quite a big turnout of boys and girls all setting off with sandwiches and bottles of tea or water. The Farmer was already in the field waiting for us to start up.

The farmer had got little hessian bags for us to put the clover in so that it dried. The job was very tedious and back-aching. Just before we started the farmer said he would pay us two shillings a bag picked. We found out that we were lucky after picking for some time if we could manage to get two bags picked in one day.

It came about that some days not even one bag was picked because the girls were a distraction. The sun was also very hot and we preferred to sit down behind the boughs of some shady trees rather than picking pink clover heads. We tried hard not to let the distractions interfere with our clover picking!

NATURE WALKS

Now, this is an episode of concerning playing truant whilst still at school and we went for a presumed nature walk with our woman teacher by name of Miss Gallager. We went down part of Northwick Park known as Dark Hollow on the way to Broad Campden. It happened to be a nice sunny morning that all the class of us boys that I was attached too was very busy with our pencils and paper writing down different things concerning this walk. Now all of a sudden without any sound or warning a big pack of hounds together with the huntsman came over the wall and road from the Northwick House side in full cry after a fox which must have past over the road somewhere close. The hounds went into the field we call Norcombe. Oh, dear, that put the cat amongst the pigeons. No sooner had the hounds cleared the road and into the field, over the wall also went half of our class of nature walkers. We went full cry after the hounds all the way up Norcombe Hollow Hill. We finished up at Northwick Hill Farm where the fox was killed. After we realized what time it was we made our way back to our separate homes.

My Mother was awaiting on my lunch. Mother gave me a big telling off and wanted to know where I had been. I told a lie and said had been kept in for not behaving. After a quick lunch I returned to school. After roll call and the register had closed all of a sudden out comes the school boss from his class room in hell of a rage. Off he started 'now all you boys whom played truant on your nature walk this morning, please step out here. I will say my intentions are to give you all the cane on each hand. Also I am sending for the Vicar to come up and hear what his decision is concerning you boys behaviour this morning'. Well the school boss tendered his intentions upon our hands and whilst we were waiting to hear the verdict of the Vicar whom had just arrived. After the school boss has explained the situation to the Vicar. The Vicar thought the head masters transactions were justified of what we deserved as punishment. Then the Vicar turned on his heel and said Good Afternoon and left. Us boys stood there holding our injured little hands and pride. But us 'rough necks' soon forgot that episode and was ready for the next truancy or mischief time.

FIRE RAISING!

Well, now this is another of our escapades which was transacted one Sunday afternoon as us boys were on our way to play football in a farmer's field called Bull Furrow up by the Warren by Fox Earths, we had to pass by two of Northwick Estates Cottages. Now I am afraid this is where the mischief started again, because just before we got to the cottages, one of the men from one of the cottages left his house and entered one of the outside vault toilets, so we thought we would surprise him. So, we waited for him to settle down to undertake his business, then we crept up behind the toilet which had a small door in the back wall, we quietly opened the small door and as luck had it one of the boys happened to have some matches in his possession (as we used to have a smoke). A small amount of the paper and some dried grass was lit and thrown inside. We closed the door and then we ran and hid up in part of the wood above the toilets and awaited results. We did not have to wait long before there was a hell of a noise coming from inside the toilet then open comes the door and out comes the old man with his shirt tail on fire a bit and his trousers down around his feet. It was quite a sight for 'sore eyes'!

He managed to put the fire out with his hands then pulled up his trousers, goes to the back of the toilet to which the other paper in the pit was burning well. Away he goes to the house for water and puts out the fire. Now when he had succeeded putting out the burning used paper and effects, he started to investigate what might have caused the fire, when all of a sudden without any warning one of the boys let out a very loud sneeze. Ho, that of course the old man heard and found out where we were hidden. He turned round quickly into the direction from where the noise came from and then started to come up the wood path to try and find us but as soon as we saw what his intentions were we were gone up over the hill and away back to the village. Now this is what happened between the Sunday and the Monday afternoon. The old man must have seen the school boss, because on the Monday afternoon after the school had re-asembled the Master had the whole school children from each class lined up in the big classroom and questioned us all concerning Sunday afternoon's misbehaviour but of course not one of the whole school was forthcoming with information, therefore that was the end of another of our escapades.

My Mother and Father taken at site of the Old Icomb Round Tower in 1986